Through It All

Promises, Shattered Dreams and Restoration

Katherine Viney

THROUGH IT ALL
Promises, Shattered Dreams and Restoration

Katherine Viney
Aurora, Illinois 60506
kathy@lifehuddles.com

Copyright © 2016 Katherine Viney
ISBN 978-1-943342-05-1

PublishAffordably.com
www.PublishAffordably.com | 773-783-2981

DEDICATION

First, I would like to dedicate this book to my wonderful husband of forty-six years at the time of writing this book. He is my best friend, the love of my life and a special gift from God. I remember the first time I laid eyes on him and heard God whisper, "This is the man you will marry." We were childhood sweethearts who have walked this journey hand in hand, though life's toughest challenges and greatest successes. He has encouraged me to follow my dreams, even when he had to make sacrifices. He has supported me with prayer and encouraged my ministry pursuits, my career changes and furthering my education. I have been so blessed to walk this journey with my special gift by my side, and I look forward to many more years of sharing life together.

Second, I would like to dedicate this book to my children Christy, Jason and Scott, and my grandchildren Ashley, Katie, Kyle, Brittany, Tyler, Hailey, Elijah, Ava, Teagan, Aedan and Keelin. They have enriched my life, and I am proud of each one. I pray their lives will be filled with the riches of God's abundant blessings, and may His grace and peace be with them each step of their journey.

Third, I would like to dedicate this book to my friend Linda, who has shared many miles of this journey exploring our adventures of faith, avenues of ministry and a friendly bucket of water.

Most of all I dedicate this book to bring glory to my Heavenly Father.

Kathy J. Viney
LifeHuddles 2016

SPECIAL NOTE

Special note: You will find references to God, such as Him, He, the and so on capitalized. This is my preference, because these words are referring to God and I want to give these words the same honor as with God. Please be understanding and allow me this preference.

My husband Paul D. Viney has written stories and supplied scriptures and prayers. I really appreciate his part in this writing journey. You will note that his name is added to the stories he contributed to this book.

Special note: When referring to scripture verses please note the following translations and paraphrases as well as their abbreviations.

- King James Version—(KJV)
- New King James Version—(NKJV)
- The Message—(MSG)
- New Living Translation—(NLT)
- Amplified Bible—(AMP)
- Amplified Bible, Classic Addition—(AMPC)
- Common English Bible—(CEB)
- Complete Jewish Bible—(CJB)

Through It All

CONTENTS

Through It All

Prayer of Dedication

I offer you my tongue to speak the Word of Life to those around me,

> My lips to voice your praise.

> I offer you my hands to do the works of Him who sent me,

> My feet to take me where you want me to go.

> I offer you my thoughts to meditate on your thoughts

> As you make them known to me.

> I offer you my ears to listen to your voice as one being taught,

> The voice of a stranger I will not follow.

> I offer you my eyes to see your fields that are ready to be gathered in,

> Harvesting the precious lives to those nearest to me.

> I offer you my heart to be sensitive to the needs of those around me,

Sharing with them the Word to sustain their weary souls.

I offer you my time to spend on behalf of the hungry,

Sharing your love and power with the oppressed and broken hearted.

I offer you my money; first to worship my Father and then to plant seed into

The Kingdom; reaping a harvest to plant again.

I offer to you, my Lord all that I am

Because you have given me all that you are.

All my love to the:

King of Kings

Lord of Lords

My Savior and my friend.

Kathy Viney
1980s

~ *Section One* ~

JOURNEY OF GRACE

Through It All

~ *Introduction* ~
THE JOURNEY

Life is a journey, not a series of events that are disconnected, meaningless, or directionless. Life's journey is step by step, place by place and season by season. Sometimes we find ourselves enjoying a peaceful rest by a gentle stream, and other times we are forging our way across a raging river. Sometimes we find ourselves enjoying the beauty of a rolling meadow, and almost instantly we find ourselves scaling a rugged mountainside. Sometimes we find ourselves gazing at the beauty of the ocean waves, and other times we're overcome by the heat of a desert sun.

Over the years I have found comfort and courage from what I call my "life verse," Isaiah 42:16 (NIV), which says, "I will lead the blind by ways they have not known, along unfamiliar paths I will guide them; I will turn darkness into light before them and make the rough places smooth. These things I will do; I will not forsake them." I like the way The Message paraphrases this verse: "I'll be a personal guide to them, directing them through the unknown country. I'll be right there to show them what road to take, make sure they don't fall into a ditch. These are the things I'll be doing for them, not leaving them for a moment."

I was talking with a friend recently who was going through a difficult time in her life. I shared Isaiah 42:16 with her, and instantly my mind focused on the perspective of blind person. I proceeded to reenact the scene, by offering her my arm. She placed her arm in mine, and I drew her near to my side as she closed her eyes. I became her personal guide directing her across the room, taking her around obstacles and describing our steps as we moved left and then right. When she opened her eyes, I asked if she was afraid; she replied, "No, because I trusted you to guide me." That is exactly what God wants to do for us, as we journey through this life. He wants to be our personal guide. He wants to walk with us arm in arm, taking us around the obstacles, directing us down the right path and navigating us along the unknown terrain. In modern-day vernacular God wants to be our GPS. What a place of confidence, faith and peace, knowing that with God by your side nothing can stop us.

When we are suddenly thrust into an unexpected horrific situation, He is there. When your heart is broken in a million pieces; He is there. When you are struggling under a heavy load and taking that next step seems impossible, He is there. It is in these times we must listen for God's voice, speak His word, and act in faith. He is there lifting us up with His strong right hand, hiding us in the shadow of His wing and strengthening us with the power of His might. Keep your eyes on Jesus and don't let the darkness of discouragement, the fog of fear, or the dense shadows of doubt blind you from His promises.

Matthew states it this way: "Come to me. Get away with me and you'll recover your life. I'll show you how to take a real rest. Walk with me and work with me—watch how I do it. Learn the unforced rhythms of grace. I won't lay anything heavy or ill-fitting on you. Keep company with me and you'll learn to live freely and lightly" (Matthew 11:28–30, MSG).

Finally, I would like to draw your attention to the four "I will" statements in Isaiah 42:16. The Great "I Am" who parted the Red Sea, brought down the walls of Jericho, and anointed David to slay Goliath promised:

- I will bring you through places you have never been before.

- I will lead you down paths you have not known.

- I will make the dark places full of my light.

- I will straighten out the crooked places.

My life's journey has been filled with desperate needs and God's provision, devastation and God's peace and failure and God's victory. May you be blessed and encouraged as I share scenes of my life's journey. I pray you will be refreshed in His love, restored by His Word and reignited with His power and favor.

Through It All

~ *One* ~
BEGINNINGS

I was born in Keyser, West Virginia on November 11, 1952 to my parents James and Katheran (Kitty) Coleman. I spent the first eight-plus years of my life in Baltimore, Maryland. I really enjoyed the big city, the church we attended, and my friends. I remember playing in the courtyard playground, making Plaster-of-Paris handprints in the Helping Hands group at church and walking on large tomato cans as if they were stilts at my friend's house. I remember my Dad playing softball with the church's team while I enjoyed my playground adventures. I always found a friend no matter where I went. I enjoyed watching the penguin exhibit in our favorite shopping center. My best friend and I walked to and from school, stopping by the candy store if we had a few pennies. Life was great, until my Dad lost his job and we had to move in with my grandparents in McCoole, Maryland.

The move changed my life forever. I loved my grandparents, but leaving my home, my friends and my church, even at my young age, was a difficult transition. First, I had a new set of strict rules: (1) never ask for anything, (2) clean your plate and (3) don't make noise. Now what eight-and-a-half year old girl do you know, that does not make noise? You see, I was now living in a four-generation household, because my grandparents were taking care of my Great-grandma Ambrose. When I think back, that must have been a very difficult season for my grandparents, but I do not remember feeling unwanted or a bother. Second, I did not fit in with my classmates at school. I still can hear that third grade teacher scolding me for anything I did wrong. She had a favorite statement, "Oh well, she's a city slicker and just can't get anything right." I went from making friends wherever I went to feeling alone, as if a shadow on the wall. Third, the place was close to a paper mill and ALWAYS smelled like stinky socks being boiled in a pot of cabbage. I just wanted to go home.

The next couple of years seemed to last forever, and I went through what would be diagnosed today as depression. I developed mono in late spring and took at least five months to fully recover, just in time for fourth grade. I had a great teacher that year who seemed to understand me, but I still felt the pressure of not fitting in. I spent a lot time on the cot, behind a screen in the hallway, suffering with headaches. They never found a cause for those headaches, but if they would have asked me, I would have told them my heart was broken, and I just wanted to go home. It was during the spring of fourth grade, that I had another experience that would change my life forever.

I was walking downstairs to the cafeteria, and as I approached the top of the stairs, I noticed a young man taking a drink from the water fountain. I heard a voice inside say, "That's the man you will marry." I decided that I had better stop and see if he was good looking. I took a mental snapshot of his face when he turned around. A trail of thoughts meandered through my mind including one that helped me make sense of living in this stinky place. If this was the man I would marry, then God had a reason for bringing me to this place. I felt a surge of hope and peace settle over my young life. During that summer I saw him again, when, to my surprise, he and his family started attending our church.

He doesn't remember seeing me at school, probably because sixth graders do not associate with fourth graders. His first memory of me came into focus during Vacation Bible School that summer. Gazing across a crowded basement classroom a cute young lady with dark brown eyes, a brunette pony tail and a green and white checkered dress (made by her mom) captivated his attention. We quickly became best friends, spending time together at church functions, later riding the bus to and from high school, and Friday nights, at my house watching TV with my parents. As our friendship developed, we shared a love for God and a passion for ministry. When Paul graduated from high school, he pursued his calling, by attending Western Pennsylvania Bible Institute, in Butler Pennsylvania, while I finished my last two years of high school.

Reflections

"O Lord, you alone are my hope. I've trusted you, O LORD, from childhood" (Psalm 71:5, NLT).

Father, you are like a shepherd to me and I know I have confidence that you will lead, guide and direct my life and keep me as the apple of your eye. You see around the corner and know the next step in my journey and will provide for all my needs.

PIONEER DAYS
(Written by Paul Viney)

According to CNN 1968 was the most historic year in modern history. The assassination of Robert Kennedy and Dr. Martin Luther King cut deep into the heart of the nation. Riots and protests over the Vietnam War divided our country and have had lasting effects to this very day.

The nation was progressing economically. The average person could buy a house for about $15,000 and pay 34 cents a gallon for gas, all on your $1.60 hourly wage. It was also historic for this young man who lived in a community so small that, if you blinked twice, you missed it. The year was 1968, and my graduation from high school thrust me into the adult world of choices and responsibilities. What would I do? Where would I go? What would my future be like?

Most of my childhood and teenage years were spent growing up in church and church-related activities. I suppose it was no surprise that I felt my life should be devoted to serving God and people. Further education was a must-have and not an option for this field of work. So the search for a school to attend and the finances to make it happen got underway. There were plenty of colleges to attend. Booklets and applications began to flood the mail box. There was just one big problem that would not go away, *money*! Education was expensive (even in those days). I did not consider my parents poor. We always had food on the table, a roof over our head and clothes to wear. But this was beyond their means of making my dream come true. I felt disappointed and questioned what I would have to do to pursue the call on my life.

It wasn't long after that our pastor approached my dad and me with information he had received concerning a new Bible Institute that was opening in Butler, Pennsylvania. Tuition was affordable, and I could work and go to school. After all, not many people have the opportunity to be a pioneer. I excitedly filled out the application; attached the transcripts, references and registration fee; and prayerfully placed it in the mail. The rest was up to God; all I could do was wait and hope. A letter of acceptance was received shortly thereafter, and I begin making preparations to attend the opening semester in the fall of 1968. Part of the preparation was to take a trip to Butler, see the school, meet the president and gather all the information necessary to embark on my theological journey.

During my childhood years I can never remember going on a vacation. The furthest I think we ever traveled was perhaps an hour away from home. Planning a trip to a bigger city that was four hours away was quite a challenge. Mom was afraid of bridges and water, while Dad could become nervous at a moment's notice. I was just thrilled at the opportunity to spread my wings and see what the rest of the world looked like. I don't recall much about the trip itself except my Dad took the longest way possible, to avoid the Pennsylvania turnpike, which he had never driven on.

Upon arrival in Butler we began to look for the address that was listed on the brochure. In my mind I was looking for a building large enough to handle classrooms and students. We drove to the Point Plaza, and all I could find was a storefront bookstore with a sign in the window saying Western Pennsylvania Bible Institute. Surely this could not be the place. How could a bookstore be the start of my theological training? As we walked through the door we were greeted by a young man who informed us that we were in the right place. My eyes scurried around the building, with thoughts screaming *this was* not *what I had expected*—a storefront school still under construction. There was a wall being framed that would separate the bookstore from a classroom. It was so secure that the man speaking with us leaned up against it and almost knocked it over. Kind of hilarious! What had I signed up for and how could this experience launch me into the ministry?

So there was a bookstore, classroom, one bathroom and a chapel. How many students would be on this pioneer adventure, twenty or thirty? Wrong—there were only seven if everyone was on board including me. This was just about as pioneer, as you could get. There was no paid staff, and the teachers were pastors who believed in the vision and volunteered their time and talents. There was no housing, so we had to find our own room to rent. There was no cafeteria for meals and no transportation. This was going to be fun! Who in their right mind would commit themselves to such a thing as this? Yet in my young heart I felt this was where I should be. Before the end of the day I had secured a room, with an older couple, who had a large home and rented out their upstairs rooms. The other details would have to be worked out upon my arrival.

To make a long story shorter, I guess things were favorable for me. I found a job working part time at EF McDonald Company (Plaid Stamp Store) and did a lot of walking. I quickly learned how to drive, purchased my first car, secured my own apartment and became a pioneer. As for my theological training, looking back academically, it left a little to be desired, but I had some instructors that had a heart to know and serve God and others with their whole being. I was inspired and given tools to work with. After all, who can really prepare you for all you will need to face the challenges life brings your way? Experience is your best teacher. How you use the tools and develop your skills is up to you.

Reflections

> ". . . *Be strong and courageous. Do not be afraid; do not be discouraged, for the Lord your God will be with you wherever you go*" *(Joshua 1:9, NIV).*

Thank you, Lord, for this reminder. Help me to know that wherever my path takes me today, I have the promise of your presence.

~ *Three* ~

HERE COMES THE BRIDE

On June 20, 1970, we were married and started on our journey. It was the happiest day of my life. The preparations were finalized as my Mom put the finishing touches on the matron of honor, bridesmaids and flower girls' gowns and headpieces. She completed six dresses for my trousseau; all made with the empire waistline, and I felt so stylish. The rehearsal and party were over, and the basement of our church was decorated for our wedding reception. A delicious red velvet cake, gifted from one of the ladies in our church was decorated and in place. Several of my aunts and ladies from the church had prepared and were ready to serve the light lunch to follow the wedding ceremony.

The day was finally here and off to church we went heavy laden with all the supplies for this very special day. We were taking photos in the fireplace room at the church, when suddenly I received the news that my soon-to-be father-in-law would not be able to attend the wedding, because he was very sick. I remember my response was, *"do we have to cancel the wedding?"* I was so thankful the answer was no; he wanted us to go ahead. I walked down the long aisle, arm in arm with my Dad, who was more nervous than I. Our pastor, Robert C. Lymburner, conducted the ceremony with a

~ *Four* ~

NOWHERE IN DELAWARE

We finally heard from the Delaware district, that a church near Dover was in need of a pastor. We scheduled a Sunday to visit the church and preach during the morning worship service. I was around six months pregnant with our first child. Our hearts were filled with excitement and apprehension as we traveled with Paul's parents on this great adventure. The church was about fifteen miles outside of Dover, and it seemed like we were leaving civilization as we neared its location. It was a hot muggy summer day, and we had no air conditioner in our car, so I will let you imagine how we felt. We turned into the gravel church parking lot and scanned the view.

My heart wilted with disappointment, but I knew I had to keep a stiff upper lip and pretend I was thrilled at the prospects ministering in this place. I knew we might start the ministry journey with a simple church, but this blasted my imagination to smithereens. I saw three buildings: the church, the outhouse and a small house. The house appeared to be, one hundred years old but was not even finished. There were no windows, so I began to imagine all the critters that had made their home in this place I might need to call home. Then the thoughts of promises made to God, "I'll go where you want me to go," began to circle in my mind as I continued to survey the grounds.

We looked at each other, opened the car door and took our next step on this adventure. As we approached the front door of the church, we were greeted by an older gentleman, who seemed excited to see us. They were getting ready for Sunday school, and I noticed a few kids seated on the front row of the church. The windows were wide open, and you could see bugs flying everywhere. There were only a few people sitting in the pews. There was a small platform and a plaque on the wall listing the page numbers for the songs we would sing during the worship service.

We took our seats on the left side of the building as the older gentleman welcomed the small congregation, made a few announcements and then indicated that Sunday School would begin. I noticed the kids and their teacher gather in a circle on the steps of the platform, as she began the lesson. The older gentleman took his place in front of a few adults sitting on the left and side of the church toward the back. There was no partition to divide the room, just two teachers, talking away and a few giggles, from the kids every once in a while.

The older gentleman was sharing his lesson when suddenly a mosquito flew past his mouth. He said, "Let me get that," as he leaned forward coming up with a fly swatter. He waved it around his face and then widened the swatting motions, still missing the bug that attacked him. He stopped the lesson and went to the back of the church, emerging with a tall can of bug spray and immediately hosed the area with its contents. I remember covering my nose and mouth so I didn't breathe in the smelly spray that saturated the already hot muggy air. As if not missing a beat, he went back to teaching right where he left off. I felt like I had to get out of here, but go where? I didn't drive at the time, and there was nothing for miles around. But I thought of one option, *"I could make a trip to the outhouse."* After all I was pregnant and would need to go soon. I thought about waiting for a real bathroom but decided it was not worth the risk, so I began a slow walk to the outhouse.

It was finally time for the morning worship and Paul shared a great message from Psalm 1. We said our goodbyes as we took one last look at this possibility for ministry. This small church was like something from *Little House on the Prairie* and yet just ten to fifteen miles from the thriving area of Dover, Delaware. I remember my in-laws questioning the prospects of taking this church. We joked about how I might have to ride a horse into town when it was time to deliver our firstborn. We didn't feel like this was God's choice for us, and after prayer there was no peace about taking the opportunity. We knew God had called us to the ministry and never lost faith that He had a place for us to serve.

Reflections

> *"And let the peace (soul harmony which comes) from Christ rule (act as umpire continually) in your hearts [deciding and settling with finality all questions that arise in your minds, in that peaceful state] to which as [members of Christ's] one body you were also called [to live]. And be thankful (appreciative), [giving praise to God always]" (Colossians 3:15, AMPC).*

Lord, I am thankful for your constant presence in my life. You handpick many wonderful experiences to show us your awesome love and powerful grace.

~ Five ~

ADVENTURES AT THE TOP OF THE WORLD

Our Precious Gift of Love

We finally heard back from another introduction letter. We were contacted by director of Home Missions, with an offer to pastor a small church in upstate New York. Paul had several conversations with the director and with much prayer we decided to accept the opportunity in Ticonderoga, New York. They wanted us to come sooner rather than later, but with our first child's due date October 23, the decision was made to wait until our baby was born and then determine our starting date as pastor.

There was a lot of anticipation as we grew closer to the due date. We were not only waiting for the baby's arrival, but the Home Mission Church was waiting on their new pastor; no pressure. The due date came and went, and although I had many weeks of the Braxton Hicks contractions, the baby was still not ready. I distinctly remember being in a Hallmark store buying Paul a birthday card, early evening on November 9; I felt something strange happening in my body. I was with my parents, and as soon as I paid for the card, we left for home. I called Paul and then the doctor. I was told to head for the hospital, and we did as soon as Paul got home and cleaned up from his day's work at the gas station.

When we arrived I was admitted, but since the baby wasn't quite ready to be born, they decided to induce labor in the morning. Paul stayed with me until visiting hours were over and then went home to get some rest. He was back early in the morning, but as I reached the time of delivery, I was whisked off to the delivery room. The last thing I heard was, "That's the head of a beautiful baby boy," before they put me under, with gas. When I woke up, Paul had a rough time convincing me we had a girl. Things were very different back in the early seventies. Paul was not allowed in the room for any examinations; he had to stay in a waiting room during delivery and was not allowed to hold our baby until we went home. Our precious daughter Christina Lynette Viney (Christy) was born on November 10, 1971, almost three weeks later than expected. Paul and I would walk to the nursery to see our baby, and the day finally came when we could take her home.

We celebrated Thanksgiving with our families and prepared to say our goodbyes. I never thought about how hard it must have been for our parents, to not only say goodbye to their children, but also their new granddaughter. It was not only our sacrifice, but they were a part of this great adventure. They would not be able to share our lives on a daily basis or see their granddaughter's changes, as she grew through the stages from infancy to toddler, toddler to child, child to teen and teen to adult. There was no internet, no FaceTime or cell phones, and land phone calls were very expensive in those days. If I remember correctly parents called once a month for about ten minutes and all other contacts were made by mailing letters or recorded letters on cassette tapes.

We packed up our 1962 Chevy Impala with our baby, clothes and a few personal possessions to embark on our great faith adventure. We were armed with strong faith, youthful courage and God's calling on our lives. Determined to go wherever God called, we traveled two days in dense fog, not seeing much past the road we were traveling on to reach our destination. I remember thinking that if we went any further north, we might fall off the face of the earth.

A wintery chill and snow greeted us as we arrived at our new home. Our youthful enthusiasm was met by three senior citizens as cold as winter's chill, brandishing their standoffish personalities and a skeptical look in their eyes. This church had once been vibrant, filled with loving people serving God, but something happened to tear the church apart, leaving these three weary, worn senior citizens trying, to hold onto a fading dream. We were told, by the Home Missions director that had we decided not to take the church, the district would have closed its doors.

We had the wonderful opportunity of standing in the gap for two and a half years, witnessing God's rekindling the congregation with love, passion and vision. The church grew from the three senior citizens to approximately eighty strong before we moved to our next ministry opportunity. God's faithfulness sustained us through those two cold winters and Sunday evening services when Paul preached to our daughter and me. We learned that nothing, is impossible with God. Even when our faith was shaky, he always provided. I am so thankful we decided to take on this great adventure.

Reflections

"God told Abram: Leave your country, your family, and your father's home for a land that I will show you" (Genesis 12:1, MSG).

Father, you see around the corners of our life and you know the twist and turns we will take, and you are always a step ahead, ready to fill us with your rich blessing.

FINDING WORK
Writen by Paul Viney

We were aware when we took the pastorate in Ticonderoga that we would need to find a job. That was not a problem. Ticonderoga was not a booming industrial town. There were very few factories, restaurants or retail stores. Now, if you are a history buff, you will know that Ticonderoga is mainly a tourist attraction. Its rich history of Fort Ticonderoga, Fort Mt. Hope and Fort Defiance are woven into the fabulous mountains and the beauty of Lake George and Lake Champlain.

We arrived in winter, at the end of the tourist season. Job opportunities were as scarce as food for the ducks. I became friends with some of the local clergy and one who worked at the funeral home put me in contact with the owner. I was to start out just doing some cleaning work, parking cars and assisting before and after services. Plans were to work me in on pickups, as it would pay more. However, my career was cut short, after just one day on the job. A fire destroyed the business, and it wasn't rebuilt until we left the village.

One of our three senior saints who attended church introduced me to a man by the name of Pete Blood. He was a stone mason by trade. On occasion when he needed extra help he would call me to tend mason. Mixing cement, carrying stone, bricks or blocks was a hard job. I did whatever was needed to get the job done. However, this work was pretty much seasonal as well.

Kathy was blessed some time later with a job at the Red Baron Sub and Pizza shop. The pizzas and subs were delicious. She was given their secret receipt for the sub sauce and sworn to secrecy and never did share it. We still have it in our possession and have used in on a few occasions.

Although we didn't make a lot of money, God was faithful to meet our needs. We believe He will bless the work of our hands so we never looked for a handout. Our motto was, "If you don't work, you don't eat." The economic times, the instability of the church's finances and the limited amount of money for Home Mission works within our denomination stretched our faith and helped us to learn to depend upon the Lord.

Reflections

"My help and glory are in God—granite-strength and safe- harbor—God -So trust him absolutely, people; lives on the line for him. God is a safe place to be" (Psalm 62:7-8, MSG).

Father, you are my source. It is you who supplies all my needs. You strengthen me in times of trouble and sustain me with the power of your Word. Thanks for being my place of safety and peace.

~ Seven ~
SHOWERS OF BLESSING

I would like to share several stories that impacted our lives while ministering in New York. The first few months of being in Ticonderoga were very difficult. That first Christmas was very hard. We had only been in Ticonderoga a few weeks. We were alone with very little money, and the gifts from home had not arrived. On Christmas Eve we found a thrift shop, just before it closed and picked out a toy for our daughter, gloves for my husband and a warm pair of brown slacks for me. In my heart I remember thinking, by the power of God I will never spend another Christmas like this again. The Christmas holidays never had yielded a lot of gifts, and most were even homemade, but being so far away from family, friends and the warmth of home was taking its toll on our emotions during the holiday season.

God heard my comment about our first Christmas, and in His lovingkindness and goodness He provided by blessing us richly during our second Christmas in Ticonderoga. A church from central New York had decided to adopt us for Christmas. I received a call from the pastor's wife asking for a Christmas list of items we needed and wanted. It was a humbling experience to share sizes, ideas for toys and items needed for our new home. They made arrangements to bring the items to Ticonderoga. As they unloaded the treasures, my heart was once again filled with thanksgiving and joy as we placed the gifts in the living room for Christmas Day. What an exciting time we had opening the gifts. Our hearts were filled with gratitude for the sacrifice made by the people we never had the opportunity to meet. What a mighty God we serve and He cares for us. God is so good.

Although the local Home Missions of the Assemblies of God was taking care of our rent and utilities, it was part of the offerings from the church that provided us with money for food and personal expenses. Connecting with the three senior citizens, being so far away from family and limited income, stretched our faith.

We had a monthly ministers meeting, and the February event was being held in Troy, New York. We took off in our Chevy Impala, not knowing the rich blessing that awaited us. At the close of the day one of the pastors said, "We would like to shower you with food." I was so thankful because we had very little in the house and trying to keep up with the needs for our three-month-old was difficult. The bags of groceries were paraded out of the church, and I felt so blessed as they filled the trunk and the back seat of our car. Our hearts were filled with thanksgiving for the faithfulness of the God we served. The car was literally heavy laden, as we cautiously traveled home.

When we arrived home, unpacking these treasures exposed the gracious kindness of all those who participated in this generous shower of blessings. There was everything—and I mean everything—you can think of to feed and diaper our baby for the next six months through all the stages. We packed the cabinets with boxes, jars and cans of food. The song writer Thomas Chisholm shared the meditations of our heart in these words, "Great is thy faithfulness, Lord unto me." Over the next six months I was reminded of the story of the widow who collected jars to contain the overabundance of oil in 2 Kings chapter 4. We had such an abundant supply of food that not only met our needs but often the needs of a single mom and her three children who lived next door.

Reflections

"Surely or only goodness, mercy and unfailing love shall follow me all the days of my life. . ."
(Psalm 23:6a, AMPC).

Thank you, Father, for meeting the desire of my heart. You blessed my family beyond what we could have imagined. Father, may your blessings be abundant in the lives of those who have sown into our lives.

~ Eight ~
SPRING SNOWSTORM

One March morning we left Ticonderoga for a meeting in Glens Falls, New York in a nice gentle spring rain. There is one thing I need to tell you, any destination of any importance was sixty miles north, south, east or west of Ticonderoga. Keep that in mind for later. Paul and I traveled with our daughter and a young lady from our church. The afternoon meeting continued until around 8:30 PM. As we walked out of the building we were stunned by the large gently falling snowflakes drifting through the night sky that had already accumulated about ten inches of snow.

It was hard to believe that the gentle rain had turned into a heavy snow storm in a matter of six to eight hours. We didn't have money for overnight accommodations or food. We hung around brushing the snow off the car, as long as possible, hoping someone would invite us to stay with them, but no one did that night. They knew we had to travel sixty miles through the mountains to get back home, but they all left the parking lot, with comments like, "Safe travels." We looked at each other and said, "Well, let's go. God will protect and bring us safely home."

Once we left the city and began our ascent up the

mountains, we noticed there were no plows pushing snow off the road. There were no signs that they had even made a pass on these mountains roads. Snow removal did not begin until the heavy snow was over, because there were so many miles to cover.

We made slow but steady progress toward Ticonderoga. I found myself pausing to pray a little harder as we approached the top of the hills, and breathing a sigh of relief, when we made it to the bottom. We were fifteen miles from home, and as we crest the top of another steep hill, we slowly began the decent. About halfway down we hit a patch of ice, and we were suddenly thrust into a tailspin. At the start of the spin I threw myself over our daughter, who was on the front seat sleeping (that was long before seat belts). All I remember was darkness, sounds of bumping and the swirling of my head, as we spun around a number of times. Paul tapped the breaks and rode out the spinning, and when we finally came to a stop with the car facing toward home.

Paul made sure we were okay and got out to check the car. The front fender and bumper, of our nice Chevy Impala were damaged, but the engine was still running, so we slowly drove the last fifteen miles home. God had safely brought us home. We traveled past the spot many times during our time in Ticonderoga. Each time we looked over steep embankment, on both sides of the road, we would pause to express our thankfulness for God's protections, because if we had gone off the road we might not be alive today. To God be all the glory!

Reflections

"The name of The Lord is a fortified tower; the righteous run to it and are safe" (Proverbs 18:10, NIV).

Father, I thank you for sending your angels to preserve, protect and keep us safe that cold winter's night.

~ Nine ~
SURPRISE! SURPRISE! SURPRISE!

We had arrived home from a Sunday morning service, and I hurried to prepare lunch. Christy was in her high chair waiting impatiently for her food, and Paul was trying to entertain her. I opened a can and threw it across the kitchen, hitting the trash can like a professional basketball player. Seconds later I heard noises coming from the trash can and wondered what was going on. I put my index finger over my lips, to indicate silence was needed. I tiptoed toward the can and took a gingerly look inside. There was the culprit—a little mouse running around the bottom of the can causing the noise as he passed under the garbage. I quickly jumped back looking for something to kill or capture the mouse that had invaded my kitchen. My husband had a bright idea, and taking off his shoe he launched it like a basketball player. What he didn't plan on, was knocking the trash can over, spilling rubbish all over the floor and a mouse scurrying for its life under the built-in refrigerator.

I quickly finished lunch, as thoughts swirled around in my mind. Where did that mouse come from? How many are living in our home? How would we get rid of the invaders? As we sat down to our lunch, we kept our eyes on the fridge, hoping not to see another mouse.

Knowing we had to set a trap we chose bacon, mainly because we didn't have any cheese in the house. We barely fried it, thinking fatty bacon would be harder for the mouse to grab and run, before the trap came down around his neck.

Once the trap was baited we went to the front of the house and settled in the living room. Christy was playing on her quilt, and Paul and I listened intently for the sound of the trap, a sign we were winning our battle against the invaders. It didn't take long when we heard the snap of the trap. We arrived in the kitchen in time to see the mouse scrambling, for his life and finally surrendering. Paul removed the mouse by the tail and took him outside throwing him as far as he could into the ravine behind our house. We decided to bait the trap again just in case we had another invader living under the fridge. Once the bacon was in place we took up our position in the living room and before long we heard the snap of the trap again. We repeated that action for several hours, until we captured a baker's dozen. We had finally won the victory over the mice in the house.

Reflections

"His huge outstretched arms protect you—under them you're perfectly safe; his arms fend off all harm. Fear nothing . . ." (Psalm 91:4, MSG).

Thank you Father, for showing us in a simple humorous way, that persistence, is important in every area of our lives. Help us to be tenacious, consistent and never give up no matter how difficult the situation we are facing. You are always more than enough.

Ten

MOVING DAY

The missons board felt it more feasible to buy a house instead of renting, so we moved across the village from Rogers Street to Champlain Avenue. It was a beautiful older two-story home on a main street and closer to the church. Our rented home was fully furnished and included a washer and dryer, but not our new home. We didn't have enough money to go to the local laundromat, so I had to learn to wash our clothes by hand. It was a difficult process and maybe a washboard would have made it easier, but I didn't know where to find one.

Have you ever tried to wring out jeans by hand? It is not an easy task. The process started by dumping laundry detergent in the bathtub or kitchen sink while running hot water to make suds. I would put the clothes in and swish them around, let them set in the water for a while and swish them some more. Once I thought they were clean enough I would empty the tub/sink and fill it again with water and a little bit of fabric softener. When the clothes sat in the tub for a few minutes, I would rinse each item under the running water and wring them out, as best I could. Finally I could hang them on the clothesline on the back porch. This process was repeated for darks, lights, towels and sheets. We began to believe God for a washing machine, and he provided the money to purchase a little Hoover wash-and-spin-dry machine through our church back home. You just never know where God's blessings will come from, but you can always have faith that he will provide.

Reflections

"It is good to proclaim your unfailing love in the morning, your faithfulness in the evening," (Psalm 92:2, NLT)

You thrill me, Lord, with all you have done for me . . ." (Psalm 92:4a, NLT)

Father, you are ever faithful, ever present and ever ready. You see the need long before we do and move upon the hearts of people to meet the need. Father, your goodness and mercy run after us.

Eleven

GRANDMA BROWN'S
BAKED BEANS

It was the Saturday before our second Easter in New York, and I was standing over a pot of beans with tears streaming down my face, drowning in desperation. There was no money in our pockets, no money in the mail and no money in the bank account. I felt like God didn't know I was alive or even where I lived. There was no other food in the house, and I was sure these beans I was stirring would not feed our one-year-old daughter, my husband and me for two days. Just in case you have never heard of Grandma Brown's Baked Beans, they were just cooked beans in a can, no brown sugar, no ketchup or any other ingredients to make them tasty.

Paul was in his study preparing his Easter sermon when someone knocked on our kitchen door. It startled me, because no one used that door except us. Paul ran to see who was at the door. It was the mason he tended for occasionally and typed his stories for ten cents per page on our red Royal typewriter. They talked about work, life and the weather for a few minutes. He finally pulled a plastic sandwich bag from his pocket and said, "I don't know why I am here today, but I felt like you needed this." I make a habit of saving dimes and then sharing them with people I think might need them. My heart leaped for joy; God did know we were alive and where we lived after all. He even brought the provision to our kitchen door. Paul thanked him and said "God has surely used you to meet a need in our lives."

When he left, we dumped the dimes on the table and counted each one, as if counting our blessings one by one. The blessing totaled $10 and back in 1972, that could buy ten times what you could today. I turned off those beans and quickly ran to the grocery store to spend this precious gift on some much-needed groceries. That Easter Sunday dinner became an early Thanksgiving celebration because God had been faithful.

God's faithfulness was proven over and over again as we served in upstate New York. I have many fond memories of our parents vacationing with us and taking them to see the three forts in the area. The beauty of the area was spectacular during every season except for the blizzard we experienced. We enjoyed watching the ferry cross over to Vermont. God brought a very special family from Canada to visit our church during the summers, and they were like a breath of fresh air. They were a younger family, that seemed to understand the difficulties we were facing and shared encouragement and blessed the church financially. We also visited them in Canada and enjoyed touring several special places in their country. Paul lost his father while we served in New York. I remember receiving the call during a bad winter storm and our trip home to be with family.

It was our honor and privilege to stand in the gap for two and a half years and watch the church grow in numbers and spiritually. We felt our time was coming to an end and thankful that God brought another pastor in to continue the work in Ticonderoga.

Reflections

> *"The Lord is my shepherd; I have all that I need.*
> *He lets me rest in green meadows; he leads me*
> *beside peaceful streams. He renews my strength.*
> *He guides me along right paths, bringing honor*
> *to his name" (Psalm 23:1–3, NLT).*

Wow, what a great faith adventure, Father. You took us by your hand, carried us in your arms and demonstrated your love and grace in our lives and never left us for a moment. You showed yourself strong on our behalf and calmed us in your presence. Thank you, Father, for this wonderful experience.

~ Twelve ~
SHORT STOP

The next stop on our journey was about six months as an assistant pastor mainly working visitation and bus ministry in Chambersburg, Pennsylvania. I was asked to work in the church's daycare center, which meant getting up early and being at the church by 6 AM to greet the children as they were dropped off for the day.

I really enjoyed working in the bus ministry, and this experience prepared us for our next pastorate. I must share one favorite story from our experience in Chambersburg. I was given the opportunity to teach a junior high Sunday school class, of teenage girls. There was a girl who attended church because of the bus ministry and who came from a rough area of town. As I remember, the class was made up of about thirty to forty teenage girls, the teacher, and one adult in charge of maintaining order.

The class was located in a large auditorium divided into six classrooms by accordion doors. As you can imagine there were a lot of disruptions and distraction in addition to this young antagonizer. We had monthly teachers' meetings. I still remember another teacher pleading with the pastor to give me additional help. But his response was always the same, "All she has to do is love them." I was frustrated, because I had tried to reach out to this young girl, but she didn't want that love, or so it seemed.

One Sunday she walked into the classroom with a new hairstyle. I went back to her and complimented on her beautiful new hairstyle. She stopped abruptly and just stood there glaring at me in silence. I didn't quite know what to do; I felt like running but waited for her to respond. Finally, after what seemed like hours she said, "What did you say?" I responded by saying again, "I liked your new hairstyle. You look beautiful today." Again she stared at me, with a mixed gaze of anger and pleasure and finally she said, "Thank you." The way that comment stopped her in her tracks indicated to me that she didn't hear compliments very often. This young girl sat quietly through class that day and did not antagonize those around her. As she walked out of class she looked my way and said, "See you next week." I never had any difficulty with her again. This experience taught me two things. First, we must remember how powerful our words can be, so we need to choose our words carefully. Second, our words can either positively or negatively affect the lives of others. We must use our words to encourage and empower.

Reflections

"Don't pick on people, jump on their failures or criticize their faults—unless, of course, you want the same treatment. Don't condemn those who are down; that hardness can boomerang. Be easy on people; you'll find life a lot easier. Give away your life; you'll find life given back, but not merely given back—given back with bonus

and blessing. Giving, not getting, is the way. Generosity begets generosity" (Luke 6:37–38, MSG).

Father, help me to treat others the way I would want to be treated. Help me to look beyond the hardened exterior and into the heart of a person who needs your love. Help me to be your hand extended.

~ *Thirteen* ~

COUNTY LIVING

Our ministry path veered west to a country community with a two-block downtown that included a bank, small grocery store, gas station and a few miscellaneous stores. We spent around five years serving this congregation of around 200 people. Since this was a small community, the members traveled from a fifteen- to twenty-mile radius. Our previous bus ministry experience proved helpful in reaching the surrounding communities. We spent Saturday visiting and inviting families along the bus route, and Sunday morning bright and early, armed with songs and stories, the driver and I would mount the blue chariot and embarked on our journey to bring them in. It actually reminded me of a familiar holiday song, "Over the river and through the woods to Grandmother's house we'd go / The horse knows the way to carry the sleigh through the white and drifting snow." We had buses going in two directions to surrounding towns to bring families to our Sunday morning services.

There are so many wonderful memories from this season of our journey. I remember loading that same blue chariot with our youth group and heading for a convention in Harrisburg, Pennsylvania. We had been traveling for a half hour or so, and the driver asked if anyone could hear a cat meowing. We all got quiet, and sure enough, we heard a cat's meow. We searched the bus, but there was no cat. The driver pulled off the side of the road and lifted the hood. Sure enough, our cat Snoopy had come along for the ride. I guess some places have church mice, but not us; we had a church cat named Snoopy. On Sunday evenings, Snoopy would perch herself outside the front door of church and as soon as the first person left the service she darted in the door and lay down on the back pew. Snoopy waited until the last person was gone and followed us up the hill to our home.

We enjoyed our years of ministry experiencing great victories, trudging through challenges and growing in our walk with The Lord.

Reflections

"You will show me the path of life; in Your presence is fullness of joy, at Your right hand there are pleasures forevermore" (Psalm 16:11, AMPC).

Father, you bless my life with things that make me laugh and pause to reflect on your goodness in my life. I enjoy being in the peace of your presence.

Fourteen

HOME SWEET HOME

I would like to provide you with a verbal tour of our home; it will be helpful with a couple stories being shared in this section. I am not sure how old the house was, but it definitely was an older country home. A carport greeted you as you pulled into the short gravel driveway. I remember the first time I stepped on the roof of the carport I was not sure the carport was a good place to park the car. The roof was shaky, scary and squashy. It would have made a nice front porch or balcony but not in its current condition.

Once you opened the front door, to the left was a nice brick fireplace, a wall of windows overlooking the carport roof and an "L" shaped paneled half wall banister leading to a partial earth basement. Moving down the hall from the front door was the master bedroom on the left and a door to the backyard, at the end of the hall. If you stopped at the steps to the basement and took a right hand turn, you would be in the kitchen.

This room was divided by a serving counter, which was made of thin paneling that was painted white. There was a two-shelf cabinet at the bottom and one at the top, both with sliding white painted paneling doors.

The countertop was covered with linoleum and a metal strip to keep it attached. As you scanned the room you noticed three different wallpaper patterns and two types paneling covering the walls. Surrounding the small kitchen were two very small bedrooms, and on the other side of the kitchen was a bathroom.

Remember the half wall of paneling in the living room? If you walked down narrow carpet-covered steps you would be in the basement. At the bottom of the steps to the right was a repair room with miscellaneous tools that an older gentleman in the church used when fixing things around the property. To the left was cement flooring where you could put a washer/dryer and a door leading to the parking space under the carport roof mentioned earlier. Behind that area was an earth floor and one part was higher to offer some support to the bathtub above.

Now, I shared the verbal tour of our home in order to share the next couple of stories that happened a few years after we moved to Three Springs. First, remember the two bedrooms off the kitchen? Since we were only about four hours from my parents, they would visit at least once a year. These stories happened during two separate visits and make me wonder why they kept coming back.

Early in the morning before anyone was out of bed I was startled awake by a loud scream from my Mom, "Kathy, come here." I quickly got up and ran toward the bedroom, where they were sleeping. There standing by the bed was my Mom and Dad looking a little wet from the rain seeping thought the ceiling. We moved the bed, grabbed buckets to set under the places that were leaking and pulled off the bedding to wash. We were fortunate that the rain stopped soon and we enjoyed dry weather for the rest of their stay. We called the older gentleman who fixes things around the church, and he came to check out the roof. In his opinion we needed a new roof. The need was presented to the board, and the decision was made to replace the roof.

During their next visit my parents encountered another item that needed to be fixed. Remember the earth floor, which provided a little support for the tub? This time my Mom was taking a bath, and I heard another loud blood-curdling scream. I went to see what was going on, and my first thought was maybe she saw a mouse. I knocked and opened the door to find my Mom with one leg on the floor and the other hanging on to the side of the tub. I asked what was wrong and she told me that when she stood up to get out of the tub, it dropped. I asked, "What do you mean it dropped?" She repeated, "When I stood up, the tub dropped." I felt it and jumped out as fast as I could, so I didn't end up in the basement."

My mom was about five feet tall and weighed around 250 pounds, so this experience was horrendous but, in my mind, it was a little humorous. Once again we called the person responsible for fixing things. He examined the tub and went to the basement and back to the earth area, under the tub and found it had dropped because the wood floor was rotting. This need was presented to the board in an emergency meeting, and they approved the floor to be replaced. I was thankful that this happened on the last day of their visit. I am sure this home was the best parsonage they could provide, but it brought a lot of new adventures into our lives along with some very special memories.

Reflections

> *"I'm glad in God, far happier than you would ever guess . . . Actually, I don't have a sense of needing anything personally. I've learned by now to be quite content whatever my circumstances. I'm just as happy with little as with much, with much as with little. I've found the recipe for being happy whether full or hungry, hands full or hand empty. Whatever I have, wherever I am, I can make it through anything in the One who makes me who I am"* (Philippians 4:10–14, MSG).

Father, thanks for teaching me to enjoy the blessings of simplicity. It is there, in the quietness of your presence, I can hear your heart.

~ *Fifteen* ~

THE GIFT THAT KEEPS ON GIVING

We were so blessed to have a family move from Florida to a nearby community. They were precious but found it hard to get to church other than Sunday morning. I remember her saying we have always been so involved in the churches we attended, but with the distance it is nearly impossible. She told us she knew they were to attend our church because she saw my husband in a recent dream. She prayed about how God could use her, and he answered her prayer. I will never forget the first time she pulled into our driveway, before church. She said, "God told me you needed some groceries." I was humbled by her obedience, and it was just in time to meet our need.

She and her sons carried a continuous stream of bags, until the back of their pickup truck was completely unloaded. I was amazed and awestruck, by the magnitude of this blessing. As I put the groceries away, it was not just stuff she didn't use, but it was everything any family would use: toothbrushes, toothpaste, tissues, foil, laundry detergent and softener and so much more. There were canned goods and boxed items, meat for two weeks and fresh vegetables.

It was like God sent this family to provide for our needs

over and over again. Great is thy faithfulness, Lord unto us. One of the times she brought food she said God told her to bring doubles of everything. She didn't know why but indicated that I would know where they were to go. I prayed, and God laid a couple on my heart that lived about forty miles from us. We loaded up the doubles, and when she unpacked the groceries, tears came to her eyes. She told me these items were on a grocery list that she had prayed over, presenting her needs to God in faith knowing he would provide. We had a great celebration praising God for his blessings and faithfulness to us.

Reflections

"Your unfailing love is better than life itself; how I praise you! (Psalm 63:3, NLT).

You satisfy me more than the richest feast. I will praise you with songs of joy" (Psalm 63:5, NLT).

Thank you, Father, I am always in your thoughts and you always has a special way to provide for my needs.

~ *Sixteen* ~
ANGELS TO THE RESCUE

My husband had returned from running errands. While driving he noticed a strange noise that he thought was coming from the brakes. He decided to check the brakes. This 1969 Pontiac was special to Paul because it belonged to his father and was given to him when he passed away. Paul jacked up the car, loosened the lugs and removed the tire. He started to pull at the hub, but it wouldn't budge. He grabbed the hub with both hands on either side and began to pull back and forth trying to break the hub free.

I was inside the house when I heard Paul scream. I came running and saw the jack had collapsed; the hub had pinned his right hand and his left leg under the weight of the car. I remember the image of a woman lifting the car with the help of angels, so I began to pray and attempted to lift the car. I quickly saw it wasn't working so yelled from the top of my lungs, as loud as I could, in hopes the neighbor would hear me and come to the rescue. I believe the angels lifted up that hub enough for Paul to remove, his hand and foot, before the neighbor came on the scene. He helped get the car jacked up and blocked. We helped Paul get up and into the house, but the only sign of this accident were the indentations made by the gravel on his hand and a little swelling on his leg.

Reflections

> *"For he will order his angels to protect you wherever you go. They will hold you up with their hands so you won't even hurt your foot on a stone" (Psalm 91:11–12, NLT).*

Father, you keep me hidden in the shadow of your wings, and there I am protected from the calamities of life. You truly are my refuge and the place I run to for safety.

~ Seventeen ~
Prayer for
Our Second Child

I am so glad that God cares about the desires of our heart as much as the needs in our lives. I am an only child and did not want our daughter to have the same lot in life. I began to talk with God about having another baby, and for several months nothing happened. I spoke with my husband and let him know how serious I was about having another child. We prayed according to Matthew 18:19 (MSG), which says, "When two of you get together on anything at all on earth and make a prayer of it, my Father in heaven goes into actions." God was gracious, and within the next six weeks or so we conceived our second child.

Back in the seventies we did not have ultrasound to identify the gender, so we were left guessing just like we did with Christina. January 1 was my due date, but as with our daughter the baby had other ideas. I remember January 14 like it was yesterday. It was a Sunday. Since I was two weeks overdue and after so many episodes of Braxton Hicks contractions, I wondered if this baby would ever come. I played the piano for evening worship, while experiencing contractions. When service was over and we went home; I told Paul I had been having contractions all evening and that they were about eight minutes apart. He calmly said, "I will take a shower," and then we called the doctor. We lived about forty-five minutes from the hospital, and it was snowing lightly, so the doctor said to come on in. We arrived at the hospital around midnight and Jason Eric Viney was born at 5:15 AM. I delivered him naturally, and it was my first time to breast feed. Delivering naturally was an exhilarating experience, and the blessing of holding this precious young man was beyond words. God had heard my prayer and blessed us with the desire of our heart.

I must share another God intervention related to our new baby. Jason was just few weeks old. We had come home from our Sunday evening service. I needed to go the bathroom before nursing and asked Paul to give him a little water from a bottle because he was crying. I heard Paul scream for me. I came running, and Jason had strangled on the water and was having trouble breathing. He would start to cry, but couldn't complete the cry. Paul and I patted his back, turned him in many different positions, and prayed for God to help him breathe. It was so hard to see him struggle to breathe or cry. Remember we lived in a very rural area, there was no ambulance around the corner, and we knew he needed help now. Paul called the doctor to see if there was anything else we could do because the baby was turning blue. I had him lying over my shoulder and was patting him on the back when he finally was able to breathe and began to calm down. Our hearts were filled with thanksgiving for God's intervention to assist him with breathing. This young man was a special gift from God and a blessing in our lives.

Reflections

". . . The earnest prayer of a righteous person has great power and produces wonderful results" *(James 5:16b, NLT).*

Thank you Father, that your promises are Yes and we answer Amen. My hope is in you, for you are the giver of life.

~ Eighteen ~
STRANGER IN THE KITCHEN—TAKE ONE

Now I must backtrack to early January shortly before Jason Eric was born to share this next event. Our daughter Christina attended a Christian school in Huntington, Pennsylvania. Paul got up every morning to take her to school and made a second trip to pick her up in the afternoon. I was already late in delivering our second child, so after getting her breakfast, dressed and ready for school, I went back to bed.

I had dozed off to sleep but was suddenly awakened by a loud racket in the kitchen. I threw back the covers and quickly moved toward the bedroom door. I cracked the door open but couldn't see anything, so I proceeded to move toward the kitchen. The noise grew louder, but I still couldn't see what was making the noise. In a split second I thought of the mice that visited our kitchen in Ticonderoga and breathed a brief sigh of relief. Something caught my eye; there it was. The longest gray cream-colored tail wrapped around the trash can. I didn't wait to see the body hidden by the trash can. Screaming as loud as I could I ran back to the bedroom to get dressed. I kept watch on the three inches between the bottom of the door and the floor. I threw on the first coat I could find in the closet, opened the bedroom door and ran out the front door.

Now remember, it was January, and it was cold. I stood by our front door thinking about how long it would take Paul to get back home, because I was not going back inside the house without Paul investigating, finding and killing that creature. I stood there for what seemed like an eternity when one of the young guys from our church stopped by. We stood there by the front door chatting away. He never asked why I was standing outside on a cold day, and I never invited him inside.

Paul finally came home and company left. I caught Paul by the arm before he opened the front door and told him about my terrifying experience. He searched the house but found nothing. I am not sure he believed me at first. I described the long grey creamed-colored tail, but we were not sure if it was a large mouse, a rat or some other creature, that had found its home in our house. I made him check out the basement area too.

I was perplexed about where this creature could have gone, but I knew what I saw. Our basement was open, and you could look down into the basement from the living room. There was a half wall on two sides of the opening and a gate that closed off the top of the steps. The floor at the bottom of the steps was cement, but there were two other areas that were earth floors. I still don't know where it disappeared to, but here is a spoiler, it just might show up in another scene of our life.

We enjoyed the bus ministry and the wonderful people who attended the church. This ministry offered me opportunities to teach adults and children. I developed a children's program for midweek called Kids' Crusaders.

I played the piano for worship and directed several cantatas during our time in Three Springs. God's power was manifested in our services and within the lives of those we served.

Reflections

> *"Shout for joy to the Lord, all the earth. Worship the Lord with gladness; come before him with joyful songs. Know that the Lord is God. It is he who made us, and we are his; we are his people, the sheep of his pasture. Enter his gates with thanksgiving and his courts with praise; give thanks to him and praise his name. For the Lord is good and his love endures forever; his faithfulness continues through all generations"* *(Psalm 100:1–5, NIV).*

Father, you are my strength and watch over my life in the good times and in the surprises that come our way. Thank you for friends and family that come alongside to encourage and share in life's interesting moments. You are my rest.

~ Nineteen ~
MOUNTAINTOP ADVENTURE
THEY ALL FALL DOWN

Paul and I began to feel our work at Three Springs was coming to an end. Paul contacted one of the district officials to let him know we were available if any churches were looking for a new pastor. We were invited by a board member to try out at Bethel Assembly in Ebensburg, Pennsylvania. We were to preach for two Sundays and the midweek service. They always like to check out the gifts and talents of the pastor's wife too. I was invited to play the piano for the music portion of the service. Jason was around four months old, and when I was finished playing he was demanding my attention. I took him to the nursery.

The nursery was a room that overlooked the sanctuary. I fumbled around at the bottom of the stairs trying to find a light switch but to no avail. I decided to carefully climb the steps, with light only coming from the main entrance dimly illuminating, the first few steps. I got to the top of the steps and saw the outline of a small room dimly lit from the sanctuary. I could see Paul behind the pulpit and gingerly took a step focusing on the shadowy light coming through the small window. Suddenly I felt myself falling backwards landing flat on my back tightly holding on to my baby. I was stunned for a minute or two. I rose up to a seated position and shifted from side to side making sure nothing was broken while checking out my son. He was looking into my eyes, but never cried. I rolled to my side, got up on my knees and finally up on both feet, still checking to see if I was okay. I slid my foot a few inches in front of me before stepping. I needed to make sure I was on a flat surface or if there was a step. I finally bumped my foot into a step and cautiously slid my foot up the incline until I was at the top of the step. As I stepped up I could feel pain in my right foot, but I pressed on into the small nursery.

I nursed my little one and stayed seated in that rocking chair proudly listening to my husband preach his sermon. I knew I had to descend those stairs and make it back into the sanctuary before my husband finished his message and then make my way back to the piano to play the closing song. I asked God to give me strength to take each step. I stood up and turned to make my way back to the sanctuary. Through the excruciating painful steps I was determined not to share this mishap with anyone until Paul and I were alone at the end of the day. I felt foolish and didn't want this mishap to affect their decision to invite us to pastor their church.

That dogged determination sustained me through lunch, visiting with the board member's family all afternoon, dinner and back to church for the evening service. Once in the car heading home I shared what happened and the excruciating pain I had been in all day. It was silliness to think revealing the fall would have changed their minds about our being their next pastor, but I wasn't going to risk it. We returned for a mid-week service and the following Sunday. I was much better after soaking the foot in Epson salt and keeping my foot propped up as much as possible. Before the next service, I scoped out the light switch location so it didn't happen again.

We were very happy to receive a call saying we had been chosen to be the next pastor for Bethel Assembly of God. Ebensburg was situated between Altoona and Johnstown, Pennsylvania, at the top of a mountain. I have always admired the magnificent splendor of mountains and spent most of my life enjoying the intense colorful artistry of the seasons. For the first time in our lives we would be moving into a newer parsonage. Our new home was situated at the north edge of town on a large parcel of ground. The dream was to build a church on the property. There was a long driveway that led to this beautiful two-story home and a two-car garage welcomed us home.

Reflections

"But those who wait upon God get fresh strength. They spread their wings and soar like eagles, they run and don't get tired, they walk and don't lag behind" (Isaiah 40:31, MSG).

Father, I am so grateful that even when we stagger or fall, you renew, restore and revive us with your strength. You make us strong, cause us to overcome and soar above the storms of life.

~ Twenty ~
STRANGER IN THE BOX

We began to settle in, carefully placing our hand-me-down furniture and unpacking the boxes. There was a deck outside the dining room with a lot of steps leading up from the garage. Just off the dining area to the left was the kitchen, and directly in front was a nice sized living room. As you approached the hall to the right were steps to the front door and on to the basement. Proceeding down the hall you see a bathroom to the left and three bedrooms wrapped around the hallway. I remember surveying the newness and thanking God for the blessing of our new home.

We had a lot of boxes to unpack and decided to leave some of them in the garage since we only had one car. A few days later we were heading out to run an errand and as we got in the car Paul remembered he needed to get something out of one of the boxes. He bent down to open the box and out popped the head of a possum. Paul jumped back, shocked by the creature staring at him. I think the possum was just as surprised by Paul and after a brief stare down, he made a mad dash out of the garage. As Paul got back into the car our conversation went something like this, "Do you think that was the possum that visited our kitchen in Three Springs? He seemed to be at home in our boxes."

"Oh it couldn't be that same possum, could it?"

Several days later Jason and Christy were playing in the dining room, by the glass doors that opened to the deck. Jason screamed and ran into the kitchen grabbing my hand and dragging me to the glass doors and there staring back at us was a possum. We yelled and banged on the glass doors to scare him away, but it didn't faze him. Jason was afraid of the creature, so I pulled the curtain over the doors until he refocused on playing with his toys.

Later that day Paul borrowed a pistol from one of the church members, but the silly possum didn't show up for the next few days, so he returned the gun. Just as if the possum knew it was safe to return, the next evening he showed up on the deck by the glass doors staring, as if he wanted to come in. Paul tried to sneak up on him climbing the deck steps with ax in hand aimed and poised to throw. As he approached the top of the stairs he threw the ax at the possum. Stunned by the blow he fell off the deck never to be seen again, at least not at our house. The next day Paul noticed a little blood on the deck and felt sure the possum was injured by the blow. To this day, when I see a dead possum by the road I think of our two encounters with the ugly creature with a very long cream-colored tail and wonder if he adopted us and traveled to our new home—one of life's mysteries.

Reflections

"A happy heart is good medicine and a cheerful mind works healing . . ." (Proverbs 17:22a, AMPC).

Father you are awesome. I still find this incident very interesting—to think a possum might have traveled with us to our new home. Father, I like your sense of humor and am thankful to know we can laugh together.

~ Twenty One ~
DOUBLE BLESSING

I mentioned in a previous story that Paul and I came into agreement about having our second child. Jason was about thirteen months old and had stopped nursing around nine months of age. I remember hesitantly telling Paul after we returned from a three-day meeting that I thought I was pregnant. I was actually a little surprised, but my body was telling me that we were going to have our third child. Soon after, I made an appointment, and sure enough, we were going to have a baby. Although this was a surprise, we were very excited that God was giving us a double blessing. The nine months of pregnancy seemed to go fast. As with the other two I had a lot of Braxton Hicks contractions for a few months, and again I was about three weeks late.

I remember the day as if it was yesterday. I was lying on the couch counting how far apart the contractions were and waiting for them to slow down or stop. Paul said, "I think you need to call the doctor and let him know about the contractions." It was raining cats and dogs, and the last thing I wanted to do was take a thirty-minute ride to Johnstown, Pennsylvania, just to be told it was false labor and to go back home. I reluctantly dialed the number and heard a voice say I should come to the hospital. We took Christina and Jason to their sitters and took off for the hospital. They checked me out for several hours and finally decided to admit me with the determination that the baby would not be born until tomorrow late morning. I am not sure how they came to that conclusion, but at 2:13 AM Scott Paul Viney came into our lives. God had given us a double blessing, and we are so thankful for our three wonderful children.

Reflections

"Children are a gift from the Lord; they are a reward from him" (Psalm 127:3, NTL).

Father, thank you for the surprise blessings you bring into our lives. Help me to always be watching for your goodness and your kindness in my life.

~ Twenty Two ~
DIVINE PROTECTION

We saw God's divine protection several times during our years in Ebensburg. One time we were heading south out of town, and Christy and Jason wanted a big slurpy from the local Seven-Eleven store. Christy wanted to walk across the street by herself. Jason was not going to let her go without him. After warning Christy to hold on to Jason's hand and to look both ways before crossing the street, they stepped off the curb. We watched her look both ways, but suddenly we heard the screeching of brakes. There just inches before impact, a car had stopped. We were thankful for God's protection and those angels watching over the lives of our children.

My husband Paul shares the second story of divine protection:

Life is exciting, full of adventure and very unpredictable. The church I pastored in Ebensberg was not far from our residence, probably ten minutes max. However, it was located at the top of a steep hill on Crawford Street. Below its steep grade was the Main Street and roadway leading through the heart of the city. On any given day or time the traffic was fairly heavy.

I was the proud owner of a bright orange Chevy Vega, which the family had outgrown. Three kids and two adults in a shoe box would just about describe it. However we made it work. It was my practice to be at the church office most mornings throughout the week. This particular morning was about to become unusual, eventful and memorable. After completing my tasks for the morning I decided to go home for lunch.

I left the office, locked the door to the church and jumped into my old faithful Vega. I started the engine and began my descent down this very steep hill only to suddenly realize I had no brakes! By this time I was picking up speed and soon would be thrust into the stream of traffic with no ability to stop or predict what direction I would be able to take. In that brief moment all kinds of things rushed through my head: injuries, fatalities, how many and how bad this could end. No time for fear or panic. "God is our refuge and strength a present help in trouble." I was in a lot of trouble, and I sure needed His help. All I could say was, "God help me." Now picking up more speed, all I was able to do was start blowing my horn and put the car into a lower gear as it was a manual transmission.

As I came to bottom of the hill to my surprise there was a break in the traffic, and I was able to fly across the highway untouched, coming to stop at the bottom of a dead-end street. As I sat there in the stillness of the moment reflecting on what just happened, I was overwhelmed at the love, grace and protection of God granted to me on this day. I took a deep breath and headed home. Oh, by the way, nothing was ever found to be wrong with the braking system, and I never had another problem with braking, as long as I had the car.

Paul just told you one story about our orange Vega, and here is another occurrence. Now you must remember we didn't have seat belts or car seat laws back in the late seventies or early eighties. Paul was driving, Christy and Jason were in the back seat, and I was in the front seat holding Scott. Paul had checked for oncoming traffic and entered the intersection since there was no oncoming traffic. Seconds later, halfway through the intersection, we were "T-boned." We were shaken, but no one was hurt. Our poor little orange Vega was demolished on the passenger's side by an off-duty police officer. Once again God's mercies were upon us, and we were protected by God's power.

Reflections

"But as for me, I will sing about your power. Each morning I will sing with joy about your unfailing love. For you have been my refuge, a place of safety when I am in distress" (Psalm 59:16, NLT).

Thank you, Father, for your mercy that is new every day. You are always ahead of us looking out for our well-being. Help us in our difficult moments to find our song of praise to you.

~ Twenty Three ~
SEASON OF CHANGE
Written by Paul Viney

Upon arriving as the new pastor at Bethel Assembly of God in Ebensburg, Pennsylvania, I learned that part of my duties would include serving as the county chaplain for Laurel Crest manor, a nursing home facility, and Cambria County jail. From my youth we had always been involved in nursing home and jail outreach, but this was different. The responsibility was on me for organization, preparation and implementation of this ministry. The nursing home part came easy as I always had a tender spot in the heart for seniors.

The jail ministry was a stretch and huge challenge, to say the least. Once a month I would conduct a service in a little room set aside for a chapel. No officer present, I was left alone for an hour among the offenders—drug addicts, murderers—you name it; they were there. The worst thing I ever did as a boy growing up was cut the neighbor's fence and his cows got out. Now here I was face to face with people who had done some serious things to mess up their lives. How could I ever relate or show them their need for salvation? For some of them their salvation was to be free of the bars and chains and that was all they were interested in. However, this was not the case with everyone. One particular Sunday I had heard that the Pennsylvania State Police had arrested several members of the Hells Angels motorcycle gang. I went to my service as usual, and this big dude with long hair and a huge beard came in and sat down in the service with the other men. I was quite intimidated but somehow managed to get through the scripture and the talk I had prepared.

At the conclusion I would always give an opportunity for people to respond and accept Jesus as their savior. I was really surprised when this big hairy dude raised his hand. Looking back I can see my own lack of faith, because I thought he was just trying to work some kind of angle to gain his freedom. It wasn't until later that I had learned this was a member of the motorcycle gang. Jesus had indeed touched his life that day. He began to study the Bible, took some correspondence Bible classes and became a leader in the jail himself.

Reflections

"Go into all the world and preach the good news to all creation" (Mark 16:15, NIV).

God help me to be prepared to share your message of life with those you bring into my life today.

~ Twenty Four ~
No Weapon Formed Against Me Shall Prosper
Written by Paul Viney

As the ministry grew we took on different challenges with a new influx of people into the church, among them the warden's wife. She became a regular, and he would come on special occasions. There came a season when life became difficult in their marriage and work. Kathy and I did some counseling with the wife, and I was asked if I would be willing to meet with him. By now I had experienced a lot of growth and development in my own life. My confidence in God, his power, presence, and word was at an all-time high. I felt ready and equipped for anything. So after much prayer, I scheduled an appointment, prepared my approach to the situation and went on my way.

The warden and I had many conversations over the years, but this was different. I was on a mission to challenge and confront him with the gospel on a personal level and bring him to a decision. His appearance was that of a troubled angry man, and it was as if I was stepping into my own den of lions. I presented Christ and shared the gospel with this man, for what seemed like thirty minutes or so. When I began to pray for him something unusual took place—he told me later that as I was praying a voice told him to put his hands around my neck and choke me, but he couldn't move to do it. I left thanking God for his protection, preservation and the opportunity to have been a messenger to this man.

Reflections

"The angel of the Lord encamps around about those who fear him and he delivers them" (Psalm 34:7, NIV).

Thank you, God, for looking out for me even though I may not be aware of all that is happening around me.

~ Twenty Five ~
FRESH WIND

We had pastored this church for several years when two new couples started attending. There was something different about this foursome. They were enthusiastic and supportive, and it seemed they breathed new energy into the church. You might have described our church as status quo. We knew God loved us, the Bible was God's Word and we practiced the rhythms of religion, but these folks believed God's Word was alive, active and powerful. They often challenged our belief system. Getting to know them was exciting and audacious.

Shortly after they started attending our church, we were invited to join them for a Full Gospel Business Men's Convention in Harrisburg, Pennsylvania. We decided to accept the invitation with excitement and apprehension. I had grown up in the Assembly of God denomination and remember one time when a friend of mine invited me to be her guest for a special revival service. My mom allowed me to attend but told me to not really listen to the sermon. My mom felt her denomination was the only one preaching the Bible correctly. When I returned home my mom interrogated me about the sermon, which was odd because I was not supposed to listen. I remember telling her they preached about Noah and the flood, just like we taught. I sort of felt the same about accepting this invitation; I was excited to see what brought these couples so alive to the Word, but put my guard up against anything contrary to what I knew to be truth.

There are several stories about these couples that have remained deeply etched in my mind. The convention was planned featuring general sessions attended by everyone and breakout classes that provided a variety of subjects to be explored. I remember attending a class on the Word is Medicine. I do not remember the instructor, but I do remember he taught that we could use the Word like medicine. There was a handout filled with names of sickness and diseases along with scripture verses that could be used as medicine for each ailment. We were instructed to use the list just like we would follow a prescription given by a doctor.

Have you ever been in a place where you felt a rush of emotions screaming "Run, you do not belong here?" Well, during one of the general sessions I was overwhelmed with that same feeling. I had my shield like the police use when aggressively moving into a hot zone. The worship was strange or at least not what I was used to. There was an excitement I had not experienced before, and it appeared like these people were part of a fanatical group. I made frequent trips to the bathroom just to ease the pressure I was feeling. On my way back from one of those trips the crowd was greeting one another, and a gentleman walked up to me shook my hand and rudely said, "If you have the joy of the Lord, you need to tell your face." Something exploded inside of me but, I fought hard to keep from responding with a rude comment. I really wanted to go home, but since we rode with one of the couples, that was not an option, so we had to stick it out. As the convention continued the apprehension lessened, but questions still lingered. Was the teaching we had learned, lived and preached wrong or were we embarking on a journey of growth? We spent more time listening to our new friends as they explained their newfound love for God's Word that made it more alive and powerful in their lives. We left that convention challenged by the experience and longing for a similar experience in our own lives.

There is a funny side of this trip. We were out looking for a restaurant, and our driver took a wrong turn and ended up going the wrong way down a one-way street. He was so embarrassed especially since he was a Driver's Ed teacher at our local high school. He cautiously backed out of the one-way street and asked that we tell no one about his mistake. Since he and his wife have gone home to heaven I don't think he would mind if I shared that story.

Our church was filled with many special people that touched our lives in so many ways. There were those who worked side by side as teachers and leaders in the church. There were others that offered to care for our children when attending meetings and performing other pastoral duties such as visitation in home and in the hospital. Volunteers helped with VBS and other church events. There was a special lady who cautiously began to attend services. I remember our first visit to her trailer and the start of a journey I am sure she never expected to happen to her. She planned to move from that trailer and purchase a new one. She asked me to go trailer shopping with her, which was very interesting.

She made her choice, and after it was delivered, I offered to help her prepare for move-in day. I think we were in the guest bedroom, and I was helping her clean the walls. We were both up on something trying to reach the highest points. We went up and down many times wetting the rags and washing the walls. To my surprise on the next descent my foot landed into a bucket of water rather than the floor. My friend was down while I was up and she moved the bucket without my knowledge. I was drenched from knee to foot including my shoes, but we had a wonderful time laughing. I think it would have made a wonderful skit on the *I Love Lucy* show. Linda has been a co-worker, co-creator, walking partner, prayer partner and special friend for over thirty years.

Reflections

"Again he said, 'Peace be with you. As the Father has sent me, I am sending you.' Then he breathed on them and said, 'Receive the Holy Spirit'" (John 20:21–22, NLT).

Thank you for always being a step ahead providing a fresh breath for a new work

~ *Twenty Six* ~
FEAR OF DRIVING
NEVER TOO LATE

I have battled fear in many areas of my life, but while in Ebensburg I smacked right into a new challenge that I had never faced during my life. I had managed to get through my life without *driving*. Yes, I said *driving*. My high school Driver's Ed class was full. They started an evening class, but my Dad's work schedule would not allow time for him to take me to class. It was no big deal for me; neither my Mom nor my Grandmother drove. It was really kind of nice because my husband drove everywhere, and that meant we were able to spend more time together. My father-in-law even gave me a driver's license for the back seat—not that I gave anyone instructions on how to drive. When my father-in-law passed away we all noticed how difficult it was for Paul's mom to manage without having a driver, but I kept pushing the idea off until a more appropriate time. After all, my Mom and Grandmother did just fine without driving, and so could I. During our time in Ebensburg Paul began to mention how important it was for me to learn to drive. I think it was really because we had a Driver's Ed teacher in our church, but little did I know how important it would be to our future.

I reluctantly gave in, and soon it was time for me to get behind the wheel with our Driver's Ed instructor. I was glad my first lesson was using his Driver's Ed car with a brake on the passenger's side. He gave me a few instructions, like how to start the car, the importance of using your mirrors and watching the license plate of the car in front, so I didn't veer to the left or right. I don't think my first driving experience lasted more than an hour and his part was over, and now it was up to me to practice. I was thankful for my husband's willingness to take me driving and for a sweet patient lady from our church who provided additional instruction. I was a nervous wreck every time I was behind the wheel. My heart raced, my body trembled and my stomach turned flip flops every time a car was coming toward me or came up behind me. I was afraid and panicking. I remember one time we were traveling to Harrisburg for a meeting and I drove a whole twenty minutes. I pulled off the side of the road saying, "I would be fine if there were no cars on the road." I finally built up enough courage, faith and experience, to take my driver's test. I passed, but the police officer said it was unusual for anyone to miss the question on alcohol and driving. I told him I did not read that portion of the book because I didn't drink. I could see from his reactions he didn't believe me, but I walked away with my driver's license. In my early thirties I finally accomplished a major milestone of a teenager. Nothing is impossible when you stop the fear and take a step of faith.

Reflections

"Don't fret or worry. Instead of worrying, pray. Let petitions and praises shape your worries into prayers, letting God know your concerns. Before you know it, a sense of God's wholeness, everything coming together for good, will settle

you down. It's wonderful what happens when Christ displaces worry at the center of your life" (Philippians 4:6–7, MSG).

Father, I am so thankful for your patience and understanding, when we are struggling, to let go of fear and step out in faith.

~ Twenty Seven ~
THE VISION CALLS

The normal view from my dining room window faded as I stared at the north edge of our city. As the scene changed I found myself peering at a blazing fire. I remember feeling a strong presence of God as I looked at this image. Intense flames of fire were leaping high, and I began to hear voices screaming "Help me please help me" as the fire tightened its grip around them. The figures were fighting the force that kept pulling them deeper into the flames. It was like they were being pounded by the waves, and they were coming up for air. It seemed at times they were winning the fight as they would surface reaching out for someone to take their hands and pull them to safety. I recognized a few of these figures while others were complete strangers. The screams for help were hellish and horrific, almost deafening.

I starred at this scene until the images faded and sounds could no longer be heard. My tears flowed uncontrollably, and I fell to my knees in prayer asking God to reveal the meaning and let me know what he wanted me to do. As I prayed and revisited the scene, I believe God shared the following message. I heard in my spirit that the things I had just witnessed were going to affect my life as I continued my journey. People we rub shoulders with every day need to be touched with God's love, power and His Word. John 3:16, (KJV), "For God so loved the world that He gave His only begotten Son that whosoever believeth in Him would not perish, but have everlasting life." I believed God was letting me know that I needed to see people around me through His eyes and reach out to draw them to Jesus. As Christians we often find ourselves cocooned within the four walls of the church, practicing our rhythms of religion and focused on our own struggles instead of focusing on the field needing to be harvested. Isaiah 58 and 61 became my vision for ministry.

Reflections

"Where there is no vision, the people perish. . ." (Proverbs 29:18, KJV).

Father, today I offer the members of my body as a living sacrifice, and act of worship and dedication unto you. Today, may my life bring you joy and praise. Father, live big in me and do your work in and through me.

~ Twenty Eight ~
WHERE HE LEADS
I'LL FOLLOW

I shared this vision with my husband and friend Linda. The more we prayed, meditated on God's Word and shared what was being revealed, the stronger this dream grew. We even allowed our imagination to take off in the vast possibilities of ministry from a teaching and outreach center to feeding the hungry and providing shelter for those who had lost their way. It was a dream we believed would take us outside the church, to become an oasis for those needing rescued from the prison of bondage, depression, despair and broken by the storms of life. This dream grew inside our hearts until it became a force to follow wherever it would lead us.

God brought a stranger into our lives. We believed the connection was orchestrated by God, and it took us half way across the county to Charles City, Iowa to a young minister from Davenport Iowa. There was such a kindred spirit between us as we shared what God was doing in our lives and ministry. He came back to our church several times, and our congregation enjoyed his ministry. God had been stirring our hearts since the vision, and we felt a change was coming. We had been praying for God to guide our steps and lead us to a place where this vision for ministry would take place.

This new friend began to encourage us to pray about moving to Iowa and pastoring this Bible study group in Charles City, Iowa. They called their ministry "Speak the Word Fellowship" and hoped to become established as a church.

We made a quick trip to Charles City, Iowa to meet with this small group, ministered in their Sunday service and checked out the city. It was the end of August, and we needed to make this decision before we enrolled Christy, Jason and Scott in school. Paul, Linda and I prayerfully took off for Iowa to see if this was where God was leading us. We met with a group of family members over dinner and shared our heart and ministry experience and their desire to have a church and how they had arrived to this point. After we ministered in the Sunday service, answered their questions and prayed, we felt God confirm in our hearts that this was the next step in our ministry. We scoped out the school and enrolled Christy and Jason. When it came to our younger son they wanted us to wait another year because of his July birthdate. We explained our situation and the promise we made to Scott was that he would be able to start school in September. They reluctantly enrolled him with stern instructions, that he must learn how to tie his shoes before he could attend. He always wore Velcro sneakers, but we knew he was up for the task.

There was one more important item our list, and that was a place to live. We were looking for a house that our family and Linda could live in together for a while. We saw an ad in the paper for a farmhouse in Ionia, Iowa. The owner met us at the house and we decided it would work for us. God had put all the pieces together, and with faith, courage and excitement in our hearts we decided to make the move. We believed this city would be the place where we would see the dream become reality. We went back to Pennsylvania and tendered our resignation, packed up the family along with Linda and headed west to the land of the unknown.

I remember leaving the nursing home where we had served as chaplain for the last time. I enjoyed making a difference in their lives as much as the blessing they were in my life. In my thoughts, I whispered this prayer, *"If I need to work somewhere I would enjoy working with seniors."* Little did I know how fast that simple whispered prayer would be answered.

Reflections

"See, I am sending an angel before you to protect you on your journey and lead you safely to the place I have prepared for you" (Exodus 23:20, NLT).

Father, I know you will lead me and guide me all the days of my life. You will turn my darkness into light so I can see which path to take. Thank you for walking through this life's journey with me. Help me to see and follow your footsteps each day of my life.

~ Twenty Nine ~
WESTWARD BOUND

Empowered with faith, filled with excitement and strengthened with courage we left fifteen years of ministry with the same denomination to pursue a vision, a dream and a journey. We packed up a U-Haul and two cars with three adults, three kids, two dogs and all our possessions, saying good bye to our home, our congregation and the mountains we had enjoyed all our lives.

The trip took two days, with stops in Indiana and finally our new home in Iowa. We encountered our first traumatic experience on our way through Ohio. Now before I tell this story, you must remember this was back in 1985. We did not have the convenience of cell phones. I had not been driving too long, but quickly realized that learning to drive was a part of God's plan for me. Paul took the lead in the U-Haul, I followed in our car and Linda was right behind us. We had stopped for a bathroom break, and Paul said, "I am going need gas soon. I am going to stop at the next exit and I will catch up with you." Linda and I did not need gas, so we got back on the road knowing Paul would catch up with us within a half hour. We drove for several hours or so without hearing a beep, beep as Paul passed or came up behind us. I pulled ahead of Linda and motioned to get off at the next rest area. I was really getting nervous about what might have happened to them, so we waited for maybe a half hour. Now, I began to think we had missed him and he might be ahead of us, so we got back on the road. The more miles we drove the more fearful I became, and my fear-filled mind was picturing Paul and our son injured or—even worse—killed from an accident. I guess I had not learned my faith lesson from Ebensburg!

I noticed another rest area and got Linda's attention, and we pulled off. We stood for a few minutes searching for change to use the pay phone. I noticed a police officer pulling into the rest stop and my heart began pounding with fear. He must be looking to us to share the bad news. I was just getting ready to walk toward the police car, when suddenly out of nowhere a U-Haul pulled up, and it was Paul. I was so happy to see him, but concerned about what had kept them. When he got off there was no gas station, and he had to drive a ways to find one, before getting back on the interstate. We laughed, sighed with relief, paused to thank God and hit the road again. I learned an important road trip lesson stay together and was reminded to pray instead of allowing fear to take over.

Two days later we pulled into the driveway of our new home. It was about five miles from Charles City, Iowa on a small farm, in a country community called Ionia. The kids were excited and ran to survey our new home and pick out their rooms. As I remember the house had a large kitchen, dining room, living room and smaller sitting area on the first floor and three bedrooms, one bathroom and a larger master bedroom on the second floor.

Reflections

"The steps of a good man are ordered by The Lord . . ." (Psalm 37:23a, KJV).

Thank you, Father, for directing us on this great faith journey. I am so grateful for your patience, your power and your provisions.

~ Thirty ~
UNWANTED VISITORS

We were busy settling into our new home in the country. The kids enjoyed the wide open space to ride bikes, play games and explore. I was adjusting to being without a dishwasher and finding the right place for our belongings. After tucking the kids into bed, Paul and I closed our door, got into bed and snuggled under the covers. A deep sigh of exhaustion gently led us to sharing the events of our day. Our conversation was interrupted by the loud obnoxious intrusive chirping of a cricket somewhere in the room. We jumped out of bed, turned on the lights and began our search for the varmint. We looked in every nook and cranny, but no cricket could be found. We decided to turn out the lights and try to sleep, only to have the same loud obnoxious chirping of this cricket. Somehow we drifted off into restless sleep, until the bright morning sun pierced its glory into our room.

The inhabitants of the house began to stir and a new day was about to begin when we heard a screeching scream coming from the bathroom. Paul and I ran to see what was going on and to our amazement we saw a cricket in the toilet. There the midnight intruder appeared to be taking his morning swim. This was the first of many sightings of these creatures. Dusty (Linda's dog) enjoyed eating these varmints, but not fast enough. It seemed like they were everywhere and for a few weeks I thought we had moved to Egypt during the time of the plagues. I guess that's what you get when you move to the county during harvest time.

We only lived in Ionia for about two months, but long after the crickets left. The more we drove the country roads, the more we realized that we needed to be located in Charles City. We checked the paper and found a duplex available on the edge of town that fit our budget. This allowed us to be closer to the kids' schools, people from the church and shopping. It was a good move and a nice home for our family.

Reflections

"Let every created thing give praise to the Lord, for he issued his command, and they come into being" (Psalm 148:5, NLT).

"Beast and all cattle, creeping things and flying birds!" (Psalm 148:10, AMPC)

Let them praise and exalt the name of the Lord, for His name alone is exalted and supreme! His glory and majesty are above earth and heaven!" (Psalm 148:13, AMPC)

Father, I really never thought of the cricket's chirping, as praise to you. Help me to realize I am just adding my praises to a mighty army of praises both from the people you created and the sounds of nature. Help me to pause and listen to the sounds that make a joyful noise. To you be all the praise, glory and honor.

~ *Thirty One* ~
ROADBLOCKS
AND GOD'S PROVISION

God had blessed us with enough money to see us through the first couple months, but it was quickly running out. Paul began to put out applications and when he was called for interviews, there were more than a hundred people showing up for a few jobs. He passed the test to become a licensed life insurance agent, but he decided he was not a salesman. Charles City was a hard place to find a job in those days. Several manufacturing businesses had closed down, and many people left the area.

Remember the whispered prayer I made while leaving the nursing home in Ebensburg? Well, Charles City was blessed with five nursing homes. I decided to see if they had any jobs available. I was most interested in an activity position, but found the only openings available were for Certified Nurses' Aides. The timing was perfect because there was a CNA class starting soon in Waverly, Iowa. Linda and I both signed up for the class, so we could work at Salisbury Baptist Iowa Nursing home. It was a six-week course, so we would begin working just before the holidays. Although this was not a job of choice, God's faithfulness and favor was upon us. Psalm 37:4 (AMP) says, "Delight yourself also in the Lord and He will give you the desires and secrets petitions of your heart." While seeking God about this move I presented a few desires. We were living in a newer home in Ebensburg, and I requested a nice home, but I should have asked for no crickets. I also asked God to provide finances to pay our bills each month. Although I as working as a CNA the pay was not always enough to buy groceries, pay the bills and meet all our family's needs. I told Him the first month He didn't supply for our needs I would know it was time to make a move, and for one solid year all our needs were supplied.

Reflections

> *"The way of the righteous is like the first gleam of dawn, which shined ever brighter until the full light of day" (Proverbs 4:18, NLT).*

Thank you, Father, for always making a way and providing for all our needs. We are greatly blessed and highly favored. To God be all the glory.

~ Thirty Two ~
ANGELS ON ASSIGNMENT

Linda and I enjoyed our trips to Waverly twice a week for our CNA classes. As a young girl I knew I wanted to help people, and I have always enjoyed being with seniors, but this was a whole new area. Nurses' aides have a very difficult job that is both physically demanding and emotionally draining. I quickly learned that it was much more then visiting with them, singing to them and listening to their stories. The job included some of those elements, but did you ever try to give an elderly heavy set person a bath in a big stainless steel tub that you had to use a scary lift to get them into the tub? Did you ever try to give a dementia resident little sips of prune juice? You thought they were drinking the juice but when they had enough, it was all over the front of your white uniform and you only had two! Learning how to care for their physical needs: bathing, dressing, feeding and getting them to the bathroom was back-breaking and nerve-racking at times.

We used these trips to discuss the latest work experience, passing the next test and the future of the vision and what God is doing in our lives. One night in early November we started our trip to Waverly in a steady rain. When the class was over four hours later we stepped out into an unexpected parking lot, very much like a skating rink. The steady rain had turned into an icy mess. We gingerly walked to our parked car and started for home. As I remember, our conversation was filled with stories of God's goodness and dreaming about the vision we were here to see come to pass.

Linda was driving slowly to navigate the icy roads, and as we were talking, I noticed what I called "a stupid truck driver" begin to pass Linda's Dodge Omni. Suddenly we felt a bump on the driver's front door that pushed us off the road into a ditch as the tractor and trailer jackknifed in front of us. We came to a stop tilted front-first into the ditch. We looked at each other, discovered we were okay and began to praise God, for His divine protection.

Linda got out of the car, to see what the damage had been done to her front door. It appeared like a fist-size slight indentation was all that could be found. We knew that indentation could not have been made by the truck as he passed and began to talk about how our angels must have bumped us off the road and what might have happened without that angelic intervention. The truck driver was okay and slowly walked toward us to make sure we were okay and let us know he called the police. When the police showed up I asked him to call Paul and let him know what happened and that we were okay. Linda was concerned about getting out of the ditch, but when the time came she was able to back right out of the ditch. To God be all the glory!

Reflections

"Thou art my hiding place; thou shalt preserve me from trouble; thou shalt compass me about

with songs of deliverance" (Psalms 32:7, KJV).

Thank you, Father, for sending our angels to surround us in this hazardous situation. You were aware of our need, even when we didn't know what was about to happen. Thank you, for filling us with the joy of the Lord in the midst of this ice storm.

~ *Thirty Three* ~
THE LORD
WILL MAKE A WAY

We finally graduated from Iowa Hawkeye University class and became Certified Nurses' Aides and employees of Salisbury Nursing Home. I worked all three shifts, but my favorite was second shift. I enjoyed tucking them into bed rather than waking them up in the wee hours of morning.

During my time at this nursing home, I found out that during a blizzard the police would pick you up and take you home or at least close to home. We had the opportunity to experience an Iowa blizzard, but when the policeman did not feel safe to go the last two blocks he told to me get out and walk. I could not even see my house until I was a few feet away, and then I had to walk further, because the sidewalk had about two feet of snow. I finally arrived at my front door exhausted and out of breath. It was the longest two blocks I ever walked.

I also learned that if a friend drops your keys down the elevator shaft the janitor can retrieve them the following day. I developed a passion for working with seniors devastated by dementia and Alzheimer's. I could write a book about my experiences working as a CNA and that training led me to a thirty-year career working in the senior industry. God is faithful even when you don't know why certain things happen on your life's journey. God has a way of working things out, for our good.

Although working at the nursing home was full of challenges, God strengthened us for the job. In our hearts we knew this was not what we came to Iowa to accomplish. The dream was burning in our heart, but it seemed our ministry time was limited. Linda and I would often walk and talk about other ways we could secure an income and have more time for the work of the ministry. We tried purchasing the materials to make wooden clowns, but between the endless hours and monetary investment, it didn't pay at all. We actually started clowning around as Winkles and Petunia. We held a birthday party for my son Scott and a family from the church.

We also bantered around the idea of going into a business. We surmised it would provide income, provide a service to community and provide an opportunity for ministry. I made a delicious pizza sauce, so we thought of establishing Barkey's Pizza Parlor. Barkey was a full costume character and part of our kids ministry in Ebensburg, Pennsylvania. We even looked at a building that would have accommodated the pizza parlor and a room in the back for the church to grow. After prayer we did not have peace about making that decision. We continued working in the nursing home and dropped the creative ideas to provide income. That year in Charles City, Iowa was an adventure in faith, and God proved faithful to his word on more than one occasion.

Reflections

"The Lord says, 'I will guide you along the best pathway for your life. I will advise you and watch over you'" (Psalm 32:8, NLT).

Father, thank you, for giving us wisdom, in our times of decision and for showing us the path to take. Help us to always seek your face, trust you and listen for your voice.

~ Thirty Four ~
SPECIAL DELIVERY

There is one story that still amazes me every time I think about it. I do not remember the exact amount of money that was needed but I think it was over $200, and God sure came through in a special way. God used a lady from one of the churches we had pastored in Pennsylvania. Her husband did not attend church with her. I remember a conversation when she had been impressed to tithe but knew he would not allow it. As she prayed about tithing God impressed her to tithe on her grocery money, and she was obedient. I do not remember her ever being led to give us money during our years of ministry in that church.

Fast forward seven years, and we had presented our need for a certain amount of money to pay that months bills. We prayed to God by faith being confident that he would supply our every need. The day that amount was needed we received a letter from this precious lady. She told us that God had laid it on her heart to send us this check, and it was for the exact amount that we had requested from God.

Now, when I think back to the precise timing that God had to use to orchestrate the provision of this need, it proves to me once again that God is always working behind the scene and knows our need long before we ask. At that time, letters took about a week to get halfway across the county; remember she lived in Pennsylvania and we were in Iowa. He had to lay it on her heart and make sure she had the money to send. Wow, what a wonderful God we serve. There was another time when a couple that visited one of our churches in Pennsylvania we had become good friends with came to visit us in Iowa. They felt led to give us a financial blessing that was just what we needed to meet our bills that month.

Reflections

"*For the Word of the Lord holds true, and we can trust everything he does*" *(Psalm 33:4, NLT)*.

This special delivery still causes me to stop and thank you, Father, for all the things you put in place for us to receive the check at just the right time. Help me to always listen and be ready to meet the need in someone else's life. Help me to be at the right place, at the right time ready to do your will.

~ *Thirty Five* ~
THOUGH THE VISION TARRY WAIT FOR IT

One year after we moved from Pennsylvania we were unable to meet the monthly bills. At the same time we received a call to become an Associate Pastor at a church in Aurora, Illinois. After much prayer and consideration we accepted the opportunity. In many ways we left disappointed and with heavy questioning hearts. Why had God brought us so far from home? Why did we not see the dream even bud toward fruition? Why did this new opportunity come our way at just the right time? I believe these questions linger in our mind to this day. One thing I believe with all my heart is found in Psalm 37:23–24 (NIV), "The Lord makes firm the steps of the one who delights in Him; though he may stumble, he will not fall, for The Lord upholds him with his hand." Another foundational verse in my life is found in Proverbs 3:5–6 (NIV), "Trust in The Lord with all your heart and lean not on your own understanding; in all your ways submit to Him, and He will make your paths straight."

Charles City was a beautiful town with a picturesque river flowing in the middle and an old fashioned swinging bridge that we ventured out on a time or two. Our family made lasting friendships with several families that we have stayed in touch over the years.

Although it was not an easy part of our journey I must say His power was made perfect in our weakness, His grace was always more than enough, and His strength empowered us to walk with Him each step of each day. We went to Charles City with the thought that this was the place the dream would happen but never considered it might have been a step, not the destination. God is always faithful!

Reflections

> *"And then GOD answered: 'Write this, Write what you see. Write it out in big block letters, so that it can be read on the run. This vision-message is a witness pointing to what's coming. It aches for the coming, it can hardly wait! And it doesn't lie. If it seems slow in coming, wait. It's on its way. It will come right on time'"* *(Habakkuk 2:2–3, MSG).*

I will wait patiently, expectantly and fully persuaded that God will bring the vision to pass, in His time. Until then we need to pray about the vision, listen to His voice and lean into that vision by doing whatever your hands find to do and walking wherever He leads.

~ *Thirty Six* ~
WILDERNESS WANDERINGS
ARDUOUS QUESTIONING

Once again we were excited about this new opportunity, although our hearts were left questioning this call God had placed in our hearts. The church rented a three-bedroom apartment in a complex close to schools and not far from the church. It was small compared to the duplex we just occupied but nice. I felt bad for the kids starting a new school two years in a row, but they were resilient and began to make new friends and acclimate to school.

Since Paul's position was part time, I began to look for work. God was already a step ahead. A member of the congregation was the assistant director of nursing at a local nursing home and within two weeks I was once again working as a Certified Nurses' Aide. Shortly after, a position opened up in the occupational rehab department, and I became a Certified Rehab Assistant. I really enjoyed working with the residents on a one-to-one basis; leading them in individual and group exercises and seeing the little improvements was very satisfying.

The dream was still tugging at our hearts with great intensity, but the business of work, ministry, family and acclimating to our new life, took priority. In those quiet times I had many prayerful conversations with God about His plan for our lives. About eight months later Paul and the senior pastor were meeting, and he was notified that the senior pastor would be leaving the church. He was actually moving to a church very close to where we lived in Pennsylvania. He told Paul that the denomination offered to help us find another church, because it was their practice not to move an associate pastor into the senior position. We decided to decline the offer and see what God had in store for us in Aurora.

God always sees the need before we do and was working behind the scene to open a door for Paul's employment at the Aldi warehouse in Batavia. It had been a long time since Paul had worked at Plaid Stamps during his years at Western Pennsylvania Bible Institute. God was always faithful to supply our needs through the ministry or His obedient followers.

God's grace strengthened Paul as he transitioned from ministry to a secular job. But questions continued to bombard our minds. Why did we leave a flourishing church only to find ourselves working in secular jobs and not in full-time ministry? Did we make a mistake leaving Ebensburg? Should we have stayed in Iowa longer? Why are we not seeing the dream/vision come to pass in our lives? What did we do wrong? But with all the questioning we were willing to be faithful servants and do whatever our hands found to do and do it with all our hearts.

We continued to seek God's direction for ministry and made ourselves available to serve where needed. During our prayer times God began to impress us with an idea for a neighborhood children's outreach program, which we later called Kid-Power. The church we were attending had some available space, and we approached the pastor with our idea. He was excited and without hesitation gave his permission to proceed.

We continued to immerse this idea in prayer, asking God to align our thoughts with His thoughts and guide us with His wisdom. God is so creative and blessed us with a powerful program, that He used to minister to children for many years. A team of over twelve puppets were created as a part of Kid-Power. Scuffles (cat) and Brandy (dog) took on the characteristics of hearing God's Word, but determined to rely on their own ideas of how to apply the message. They were always getting into trouble because they did not do it God's way. The drama team reiterated how to successfully apply God's Word in our lives, while music, memorization and other learning projects provided an interactive element to the program. The neighborhood outreach drew in thirty to forty children on a weekly basis, and it was exciting to see God at work in their lives. About two years after Kid-Power was launched we faced change. The pastor decided to sell the church, to another group of believers, and they needed the space. We moved to a different location, but the distance made it difficult for the neighborhood kids to attend, so we disbanded. We were able to resurrect Kid-Power, as the children's ministry for another church offering a Sunday and Wednesday program.

Years later I was standing at the checkout in Walmart and the cashier looked at me and ask if I remembered her. I looked closely and said I am not sure. She shared her name and a memory from the Kid Power outreach, thanking me for the opportunity to learn about God. The seeds sown in her life continued to thrive into her adult life. To God be all the glory. If we offer our lives to God, He will lead us to those who need His touch.

Reflections

"There has never been the slightest doubt in my mind that the God who started this great work in you would keep at it and bring it to a flourishing finish on the very day Christ Jesus appears" (Philippians 1:6, MSG).

When I don't understand all that happens in life, help me to trust in you because you know the beginning and the ending chapters of our lives.

~ *Thirty Seven* ~
DEALING WITH LOSS

The phone interrupted the silence, and I heard my Dad's voice, shaky, scared and overwhelmed. I could hear his tearful voice saying Mom was in the hospital and had a stroke. A series of mini-strokes had left my Mom paralyzed on her left side, and they were not certain she would be able to walk again. She was able to speak, but it was difficult to understand all the words, and she seemed to have difficulty putting complete thoughts together.

We made a quick trip home to see her and help get the house ready for her return home in a wheelchair. I stayed as long as I could and left my Dad and Mom in God's hands. They had support from family, friends and home health care. Close to three months later Paul and I made another trip to the East coast. I wanted to spend time with Mom and give Dad a little break, since the home health care was no longer present to assist with care. It was getting harder for Dad to take care of Mom. She was obese and transferring her was wearing on his strength, physically and emotionally.

At this time I was working as an Occupational Rehab Assistant and knew that with a positive attitude and some exercise she could improve and regain some of her abilities. I encouraged her, but it didn't seem to make a difference. Mom's talkative nature, contagious laughter and constant creativity had been replaced with fear, anger and hopelessness as she looked off into the darkness of a melancholy state.

It came time to head back to Illinois, and we said our goodbyes, but little did we know that we would arrive home to the tears of our children and the news that she had passed away while we were traveling from Maryland to Illinois. We gathered our children and packed our suitcases and headed back to the East Coast to say our final goodbyes.

In the months to follow I struggled with my own anger. Why didn't my Mom fight harder to come back from the stroke? I think I missed her more than anything, but I had mixed emotions of dealing with her loss.

Reflections

"He heals the brokenhearted and binds up their wounds [curing their pains and their sorrows]" *(Psalm 147:3, AMPC).*

Thank you, Father, for coming into my brokenness and healing my painful emotions, my agonizing loss and my broken heart. Thank you, for bringing me back to a place of peace, rest and joy. You are a loving and good Father.

~ Thirty Eight ~
WEDDING BELLS

We have lived in Aurora for thirty years, and many wonderful and exciting things happened. I had the privilege of having my daughter Christy work in the activity department I managed. It was a joy to watch her work with the residents and develop special connections with many that she served. She was not just my daughter but a friend and coworker. I remember the day she came back to the office and said, "I met a very special man, and I think he is the one." The young man was in the Navy and was home on a short leave. His grandfather was a resident, and they met while he was on leave from the Navy. It was love at first sight, and within three months, while celebrating Thanksgiving with my Dad they announced their engagement. Along with that announcement was the wedding date of December 21. That meant I had about four weeks to plan a wedding in addition to the many responsibilities at work getting ready for the Christmas holiday.

The time went fast and furious as we planned every detail. I was proud to have her wear my wedding dress and veil with a few alterations. She picked out her bridesmaids' gowns, and in one quick visit to the local mall their dresses were purchased. A local flower shop was able to take care of the wedding flowers, and since it was the Christmas season, the church was beautifully decked out with poinsettias. The dining services supervisor offered to bake the cake as a wedding present. Plans were coming together nicely, but I was getting lost in a mountain of emotions. I was not only losing my daughter who had become a special friend, but I was losing a valued employee from my activity department. This was my first child to leave the nest, and I felt emotionally like a volcano ready to erupt. I was alone and on my way to pick up something for the wedding when the volcano erupted and spewed out a tearful mess. Mixed with the tears were anger, grief and despair, as I tried to figure out how I would get through this season of my life. Self-pity took over, and I fell apart.

Through the noise of my despair a thought raced across my mind, "Isn't this what you raised her to do?" I was stunned as this thought settled into my awareness. As I took a few deep breaths and saw the image of an eagle taking flight, I was proud of this young lady, and regardless of my apprehension it was time to let her spread her wings and fly off to start her own life. We had brought her up to serve the Lord, and I had to place her into His loving hands to guide and direct her steps into the paths He had chosen for her. I am so glad that our heavenly Father knows just how to work in our lives and His love, peace and rest washed over me that night.

I was led to write her a letter and purchased a porcelain eagle in flight and presented it to her the night before she was married. It was a beautiful wedding ceremony and reception, and soon after, we said our good byes as she took flight into her new life. Over the years Matt and Christy have blessed us, with seven grandchildren. The first three of her children were born on the East Coast. When Matt left the military, they decided to move back home.

Reflections

> *"But those who trust in the Lord will find new strength. They will soar high on wings like eagles. They will run and not grow weary. The will walk and not faint" (Isaiah 40:31, NLT).*

Many times in life I have found it hard to let go and let God, but He is always faithful to walk us through those times if we will allow Him to do a new work in our lives.

~ *Thirty Nine* ~
MIRACLE OF GRACE

Today, as I watched our beautiful, blonde-haired, blue-eyed, granddaughter, Brittany Dawn, playing, my thoughts went back to the miracle of her birth. I will never forget the fear and the joy of that cold February night as we anxiously awaited the cry of life.

That very special day began around 1:00 P.M. Christy was overdue, and the doctor had decided to induce the labor. My daughter had invited me to be present for this birth, as I had missed the first three because Christy lived on the East Coast. I felt privileged and honored to be part of this wonderful occasion. The nurses set us up in a beautiful birthing room. I remembered when my daughter was born, the father could not be in the room let alone another family member.

Christy went through all the preparations and settled in with the monitors in place. The nurses came in with the medication to induce labor and things took off real fast. When the nurses reported how fast labor was progressing, the doctor instructed them to slow it down by reducing the medication because he was involved in an emergency C-section. Christy asked me to lead in prayer for a safe delivery and a healthy baby. Within a few hours, Christy was in great pain and Matthew (the husband), and I took turns rubbing her back, offering comfort and giving reminders to breathe properly.

I was constantly watching the monitors, noticing times when the baby's heart rate would escalate dangerously and then drop low. After observing this for a while, I made an excuse to leave the room and went to the nurse's station with my concerns. They seemed to think it was a monitor problem, came into the room and made the necessary adjustments. The heart rate seemed to stabilize and then would begin fluctuating again, and Christy seemed to be in intense pain. I felt helpless to make things better, so I prayed while trying to keep my concern from being apparent to my daughter.

Finally, when the shift changed, I was able to find a nurse who listened to my concern. The nurse adjusted the monitor and asked Christy to turn over. While the nurse was watching the monitor, the baby's heart rate repeated the dramatic highs and lows several times. They contacted the doctor to share their concerns, but the doctor was now involved with a second emergency C-section and was not yet available. While the nurses were talking with the doctor, Christy said, "I have to push," and they said, "No, not yet." That is like telling a river to stop flowing. I overheard one of the nurses say that none of them had ever been involved in a difficult delivery without the doctor being present. As the drama intensified, I began to pray.

The nurses conducted another examination, and found that the baby was coming with the umbilical cord wrapped around the neck, not once but twice. You could see the panic in the nurse's eyes as they moved swiftly into place. I suddenly became aware of a woman dressed in a lab coat. The woman began to give step-by-step directions with a gentle, calm voice, and they followed as if she were the expert. As soon as Brittnay was in the nurse's arms, they rushed over to the warming bed and began to work, suctioning, poking and prodding. We waited for what seemed like an eternity, praying, hoping, trusting in God's power to intervene and then, shattering the silence, was the cry of this precious baby girl. We embraced and erupted in a joyous celebration, for this miracle of life.

Later I asked the nurses who that woman was that gave those directions, but no one seemed to know. I asked my daughter and son-in-law if they saw her, but they did not, and besides, they were too busy. I walked the halls looking for her to say thank you, but I could not find her anywhere. I went back into the room wondering if God had actually sent an angel into that birthing room for a special mission, on that cold February night.

Reflections

"Thank you for making me so wonderfully complex! Your workmanship is marvelous-how well I know it" (Psalm 139:14, NLT).

You saw me before I was born. Every day of my life was recorded in your book. Every moment was laid out before a single day had passed" (Psalm 139:16, NLT).

Thank you, Father, for your Grace and Provision in this situation. Thank you, for making a divine appointment for that person or your angels to provide what was needed to bring that special life into the world.

~ Forty ~
BUT YOU ARE DOING
THE LORD'S WORK

At the time of writing this book we have lived in Aurora for thirty years. We have been blessed in our lives, careers and ministry. Paul worked at the Aldi warehouse in Batavia, for twenty-eight-and-a-half years before retiring. I have been blessed with three great jobs during our years in Aurora. I spent twelve years working in a nursing home, as a Certified Nurses' Aide, Certified Occupational Rehab Assistant and finally as a Certified Activity Professional. I had the honor of working as a private duty companion with an elderly lady in her home for almost a year. God blessed me to work in a retirement community for seventeen-and-a-half years, before retiring last year.

But during this time, the questioning continued to trouble my thoughts. I remember questioning whether my life was still pleasing God since I was no longer serving a congregation, as a pastor's wife. I was walking down the hall when a gentleman in front of me, turned toward me and said, "You are doing the Lord's work." I was stunned by his comment, but said thank you for sharing that with me. He started walking down the hall again, and I moved closer to going downstairs to my office. Within a few seconds he turned again and headed toward me. He came a little closer and pointed at me and said, "You are doing the Lord's work." I was shocked that he would come to me twice and share the same thing, but once again I said thank you for sharing that with me. We both started off to our separate destinations, but a few seconds later he was standing right in front of my face with his finger pointed and almost touching my nose. He proceeded to say, "BUT YOU ARE DOING THE LORD'S WORK."

By this time I was in tears. He had approached me three times with the same statement and each time with a little more force. I began to recognize this was God speaking to me in a very unusual way. You see this gentleman sat on a couch, in our front lobby fiddling with index cards and watching people come and go. He suffered from dementia, and this was a routine he followed each morning. He did not do a lot of communicating, and when he did, his comments did not make sense. I believe God saw the cry of my heart and the questioning in my mind and the ache in my heart and moved upon this man to remind me, "You are doing the Lord's work." I thanked him for sharing his comments with me and ran to my office shut the door and spent time thanking God for caring enough to send this man with His message.

I believe the steps of a good man or woman who trust God are led by the Lord. Proverbs 3:5–6 (MSG) says, "Trust God from the bottom of your heart; don't try to figure out everything on your own. Listen for God's voice in everything you do, everywhere you go; he's the one who will keep you on track." Maybe I was more fixed on the *who* God called me to be than *what* he called me to do.

When Jesus asked Simon Peter in John 21:15–16, "Simon, son of John, do you love me more than these," (speaking of the fish they had just caught)? Jesus said, "Feed my lambs" and the second time, "Shepherd my Sheep" and finally "Feed my sheep."

In Matthew 28:18–20 (MSG) Jesus gave his disciples this charge, *"Go out and train everyone you meet. Instruct them to practice all I have commanded you. I'll be with you as you do this, day after day, right up to the end of the age."*

Mark 16:15 (MSG) says, *"Go into the world. Go everywhere and announce the Message of God's good news to one and all."*

God has called each of us to reflect His love, His power and His Word in the earth. "Go ye," was God's directive to all believers! There is a world of hurting people looking for a healing touch. There is a world of people in bondage to bad habits, negative thinking and fear looking for someone to set them free. There is a world of lost people trying to find their way back to God. Although teaching and preaching are paramount, ministering to the person next to you, on the train, across the table from you, at the restaurant or showing kindness to your neighbor, is real life ministry. GO YE, INTO YOUR WORLD AND MAKE A DIFFERENCE!!!

Reflections

". . . to loose the chains of injustice and untie the cords of the yoke, to set the oppressed free and break every yoke? . . . share your food with the hungry and to provide the poor wanderer

with shelter—when you see them naked, to clothe them . . ." (Isaiah 58:6, MSG).

Thank you, Father, for sending that gentleman across my path to remind me that ministry is not just the preacher sharing a sermon or a teacher teaching the Word, but it is every believer doing the works we saw Jesus doing, as He walked on the earth. Guide my steps each day to someone who needs Your love, Your Word and Your power to touch their lives.

~ Section Two ~

THROUGH THE FIRE

Through It All

CHAOS

When we lived in the mountains back east, my husband enjoyed taking visitors on a special ride. He knew the scenic roads filled with hills and valleys and a lot of twist and turns. When he reached the top of a hill he would gradually speed up until he went through the valley area and started up the next hill. This causes what we called, "tickle belly" experiences, similar to a roller coaster. Many times life is the just like this, you crest the top of a hill and everything is going fine, but suddenly we find ourselves in the valley, being startled by a trial, difficulty or fear. You take your stand of faith and pray and get through the situation fairly easily. But there are times in our lives when a horrendous catastrophic event devastates your life, and it takes a long time to get through the field of debris and reassemble the shattered pieces of your life.

This is the account of a hellacious incident that penetrated the very heart of our lives. It was difficult to conceive that life would ever be the same again. Disaster had left our lives in ruins. How would we ever pick up the pieces and put our lives back to together? How would we ever make sense of the destruction? Our lives had become:

- Twisting thoughts—Swirling emotions

- Jagged edges—Agonizing pain

- Crushed dreams—Broken promises

- Angry voices—Deafening silence

- Taunting questions—Evasive answers

- Empty rooms—Uncertain future

Reflections

"He lifted me out of the slimy pit, out of the mud and mire; he set my feet on a rock and gave me a firm place to stand" (Psalm 40:2, NIV).

In the darkest place I know you are with me and I can trust you, to bring me out into the light of your love. I know you will pick me up in your arms of love and sustain me with your Words of life.

~ *Forty One* ~

NIGHTMARE FROM HELL

Suddenly an explosion of catastrophic proportions shattered the peaceful stillness of a star-studded June evening. Piercing through the darkness came the brightness of flashing red and blue lights and the sound of screaming sirens, as the police and fire fighters arrived on the scene. The stench of explosives penetrated the night air. Neighbors gathered near the broken window to see what was going on inside.

That evening was like every other Wednesday; I taught a Bible class at church and picked up my husband from work. Paul was hungry, so we stopped by McDonald's for a sandwich. It only takes twenty minutes to drive home and we spent the time laughing and sharing our day's experience. As we turned the corner we noticed flashing lights and assumed there was an accident in front of our house. As I drove closer to house we quickly became aware that there was no accident; something was happening on the west side of our house. We jumped out of the car and ran around the corner to find our neighbors standing around the window of our son's room. Paul and I pushed through the crowd and stood peering through the frame, of what used to be a window. We saw the firemen laden with their equipment walking around the basement and police officers demanding to know what happened. Our next-door neighbor tried to explain what they heard and saw, but panic took over, and we took off running through the back door and down to the basement. We stood as if paralyzed and stunned by the shocking scene that was unfolding. I was trembling, tears streaming down my face, as my husband held me tightly. It felt like I had been hurled in the middle of someone else's dream. I heard the sound of loud voices, as the police continued to question our older son. "Tell me why you were playing around with explosives?" Our son retorted, "Someone tossed it through the window; why won't you believe me?"

We continued to stand frozen in the corner of this chaotic nightmare as fear gripped every fiber of our being. I gathered a little courage and began to scan the devastation: beer bottles all over the place, glass everywhere from the explosion and his room being tossed by the police. The officer drilled our older son, "Tell me why you were playing with explosives and what was going on here tonight." Our son responded with a cocky look on his face, slightly slurred speech and a tinge of anger, "Someone threw it in the window like I said. Why don't you believe me? " The questioning continued, Where are the drugs? Our son continued to answer, There are no drugs. The police disgustedly shouted, "I'll bring the dogs down here if you don't tell me."

My mind was spinning, and my heart was crushed with hurt and anger. Standing across the room, I stared straight into his eyes and said, "Son if you have drugs, you better tell them where they are right now." I was so distraught and overcome with anguish I could not take it anymore, so I ran upstairs and Paul followed me. We stood there embraced in each other's arms crushed, devastated and bewildered.

Never in my life had I experience the fear and horror of those moments. Panic gripped my body, disbelief stunned my mind, and confusion engulfed my emotions as I tried to make sense of this nightmare being played before my eyes. My trembling body was wrenched with the terror, as my swirling thoughts tried to make sense of the horrific scene.

A few minutes later we returned to the basement to see both of our sons handcuffed, standing side by side against the front wall of the basement. Rooms had been searched and drugs had been found along with drug paraphernalia and a sawed-off shotgun. I stood there falling apart, when our younger son said, "Mom, I'm really sorry." My eyes focused on my older son, but his comment was so different. "Mom you are going to bail me out; you are going to bail me out, aren't you?" I looked into his eyes and said, "Son, we don't have that kind of money."

As parents we stood there stuck in an emotional quicksand struggling with anger and compassion, love and heartbreak, confusion and bewilderment, shock and numbness. The pain and hurt was unreal. Like a jagged knife thrusted and twisted into our inward most being; tearing us apart.

It was so hard to watch our boys handcuffed and ushered by the officers up the steps, into the living room and taken out the front door of our home. As the police shut the door we were left in dark silence, cold emptiness and agonizing questions. We watched out the living room window as the transfer van pulled up and the boys were assisted into the van and driven off. It was just after midnight (also our twenty-sixth anniversary) and the silence was eerie. All I could do is fall into my chair in a heap of ruin, sobbing my heart out. My husband took me in his arms and spoke these words of assurance. "Everything is going to be all right." I finished his words with, "Because God works it all together for our good and this tragedy will be turned into triumph."

We spent the next few hours in prayer, pacing the floor and swimming in hurricane-force waves of emotions. Finally around 3:00 AM, exhausted from the turmoil, I sat down. In the silence we heard a noise, but when we checked the front of the house and the back, we found nothing. I decided to go to the bathroom but paused by the dining room window. I was horrified by the new sight I was watching. Two people were inside our son's car. I whispered for Paul to look and he sent me to called 911. As if the night didn't have enough disaster; we found ourselves facing something else. The operator asked what seemed like a million questions. Paul said they are getting out of the car and running through the back yard. I conveyed that to the operator and she said someone was on the way. We waited three minutes, which seemed like an hour, and finally began to see police all over the area, but it was too late and the perpetrators had already fled the scene.

Reflections

"We've been surrounded and battered by troubles, but we're not demoralized; we're not

sure what to do, but we know that God knows what to do; we've been spiritually terrorized, but God hasn't left our side; we've been thrown down, but we haven't broken" (2 Corinthians 4:8–9, MSG).

Father, I am grateful that when our world comes crashing down and we are devastated by the nightmare we find yourselves in, you are there with Your strength, Your wisdom and Your grace. You hold us tight and never let go. Thank you, for being there in the midst of our chaos speaking peace.

~ Forty Two ~
THE AFTERMATH OF DEVASTATION

The bright sunlight of a new day pierced the wreckage of our sleepless bodies, wrenched emotions and harassed spirits. Hoping it was all a dream but knowing it was real, we had questions that began to overwhelm our thoughts. How did their youthful struggles turn into this horrific nightmare? Why did this happen? Who was involved? What did we do to plant seeds for this kind of harvest? What do we need to do next? How do we get to see our boys? The questions were endless, but the answers seemed few. The questions turned inward, and thoughts began to pronounce us guilty, *It is all your fault. If you had done this or you had done that; this wouldn't have happened.* It was hard to put one foot in front of the other or even imagine how we would survive the next second, the next minute or the next hour. And what about the boys; were they all right; were they safe; where were they? God's Word eased its way through the questions to remind us that He was there and would help us walk through this fiery pit of destruction and help us find our place of peace and victory once again.

The police stopped by and said they found tracks in the fresh morning dew, but they ended at the cul-de-sac a few blocks away. Later we received a call from the police station asking us to meet an officer in that cul-de-sac around 10:30 A.M. Someone mowing their yard found a stereo and kicker box. Paul went over to identify and retrieve the items. I often wondered if our angels showed up and scared the thieves in the middle of the night.

Later that day we became concerned for our own safety. We did not know what our boys had gotten themselves into, nor did we know if they, whoever "they" were, would come back. We decided to spend the night in a hotel; after all it was our twenty-sixth wedding anniversary. We were so blessed by the other pastors and friends from our church who gathered around us to offer prayer support and bless our home. God is ever faithful, ever loving and ever present in the good times and in the difficulties of life.

These are a few of the verses that God used during the hours, days, weeks and months that followed.

". . . I am with you all the days (perpetually, uniformly, and on every occasion), to the [very] close and consummation of the age. Amen (so let it be" (Matthew 28:20, AMPC).

"And I will bring the blind by a way that they know not; I will lead them in paths that they have not known. I will make darkness into light before them and make uneven places into a plain. These things I have determined to do [for them]; and I will not leave them forsaken" (Isaiah 42:16, AMPC).

"Trust in and rely confidently on the LORD with

all your heart And do not rely on your own insight or understanding. In all your ways know and acknowledge and recognize Him, And He will make your paths straight and smooth [removing obstacles that block your way]" (Proverbs 3:5-6, AMP).

We believed God's Word was alive, powerful and sharper than a two-edged sword and nothing and no one is impervious to God's Word (Hebrews 4:12–13). We spent years listening to, meditating on and depositing God's Word into our hearts and minds. God's Word was deeply rooted into the soil of our hearts and was our first response to any difficulty in our lives.

The next few days seemed like a blur and yet being on an emotional roller coaster as we tried to sort through the shattered pieces of our lives. The boys were in different locations because of their ages. I believe it was Friday before we could see our older son. I remember feelings of humiliation, intimidation and trepidation, while waiting to visit our son. I was upset to find out that only one of us could go in to visit, but my husband graciously deferred to me. I only had a few minutes to talk, as glass separated us from any contact. I picked up the phone and a mixture of tears, anger and compassion flooded me the next few minutes. He seemed to be okay and even a little cocky, like this was not a big deal. He kept asking if we were going to bail him out, and I said no we don't that that kind of money. The officer yelled times up and I said I love you and hung up the phone.

It was Saturday before we received a call from our younger son. I could hear the fear in his voice, but he was trying to be brave. Visiting hours were Sunday, so we were finally able to see him. Monday he was released with an ankle monitor. Later, our older son was found guilty and sentenced to nineteen months in jail.

The devastation of this horrific event shattered our lives in indescribable ways, but we held on to the words we first spoke that very dark night on June 20, 1996. "Everything is going to be all right . . . because God works it all together for our good, and this tragedy will be turned into triumph."

Although we found God's Word to be our source of strength, that did not mean it wasn't a battle to draw on that strength. Sometime the questions, fear and doubts engulfed my emotions, like waves crashing on the shoreline during a hurricane. Then scenes from their childhood would parade through my mind. Where was that son who ran around a building yelling, come quick, I just saw Jesus! When we returned to that spot, he couldn't see Jesus and he was concerned I wouldn't believe him. I hugged him tightly and told him I believed you saw Jesus and what a privilege to experience seeing Him. Where were my sons who knew the Bible verses like the back of their hand and were always first to answer questions in the children's programs at church. Where were my sons who once were so excited to be in church, prayed for everything and believed God for healing whenever they were sick? In my mind's eye I could still see our daughter directing the boys as they sang praises to God, with *Psalty the Singing Songbook* playing on the cassette recorder.

In desperation I cried out to God asking for these prodigal sons to come back to the Lord. I remembered being in prayer one morning exactly one year, three months and three days before this incident occurred, searching through Isaiah for God's Word regarding my sons. They were running as hard and fast as they could from God and his love and embracing the enemy's devices. This is the prayer God gave me on March 16, 1995, "I have engraved yours sons on the palms of my hands (I could see their names in the nail prints in His hands). Your sons will hasten back to you. They will be gathered and come to you. For those who came to lay you wasted, ruined, desolate and devoured will depart from you. Lift up your eyes and look around, they are gone. Hope in the Lord, for that hope will not be disappointed. I will contend with those who have contended with you and your children I will save. For I will take them from the hands of the warriors and fierce, for the battle is mine and you will wrap up in the joy and delight of God's provision."

Still swirling in the chaotic thoughts from this horrific incident, a dream flashed into my mind. It happened a few weeks prior to this incident. As the dream began, a tall stout man demanded his way in the back door of our sun porch. He had a whiskey bottle in his hand and was staggering drunk. I remember standing in front of him, and as I lightly pressed my hand on his shoulder, he passed out on the floor. I spoke to him with all the authority I gathered from within and command he get out of my house in the name of Jesus. He got up and staggered out the door and fell on the rocks between our driveway and the parking lot next to our home, and there he lay through the rest of my dream.

Suddenly six cars drove into the parking lot, formed a circle and waited for a few minutes. Almost as quick as they came they pulled out, one by one heading down the street. They proceeded east toward the center of town. As if each driver was in a drunken stupor or inflicting intentional acts of terror, they zig-zagged across the four lanes of traffic, knocking down telephone poles, running into houses and demolishing cars, causing one explosion after another until everything was damaged or engulfed in flames from the devastation they had caused. As I stood frozen in fear, a thought penetrated through this indescribable scene. Where was my son? I hoped he was not with them. In the dream I ran downstairs, and there he was in his bedroom. I grabbed him and said, "Thank God you're safe and sound." The dream seemed so real, but as I awakened from this nightmare I began to pray and praise God for His protection and power to be at work in my son's life. Looking back I wonder if things might have been different if I had prayed harder in my response to the dream. If I had asked for discernment, maybe I could have stopped that hellish night from happening. But on the other hand, if I had known exactly what was going to happen a few weeks later, I don't think I could have handled that knowledge.

Reflections

"Uphold me according to Your promise, that I may live; and let me not be put to shame in my hope! Hold me up, that I may be safe and have regard for Your statutes continually!" (Psalm 119:116–117, AMPC).

Thank you, Father, that I am the apple of your eye. Thank you that you can see the catastrophic event in our lives. Thank you, for holding us in your strong right arm and hiding us in the shadow of your wings.

~ Forty Three ~
DIVINE INTERVENTION
Written by Paul Viney

After our younger son was released from detention we began to notice some changes taking place in him—changes in attitude, mindset and interests. Life for him and us was in a rebuilding process as trust once again had to be reestablished. We secured an attorney to represent him, and counsel us in the best approach to this situation. There was the house arrest, ankle monitoring, visits from law enforcement, drug testing counseling, community service hours and court visits, stretching us to a new level of trusting God.

He began to attend church, focus on his anger issues and condition himself physically. Attending church was a big step for him, as he had been so hostile toward it until his wake-up call. Fortunately he was surrounded by a loving, accepting group of people who became his friends and who remain friends to this day. It did not take long for him to decide to follow Jesus, a life-changing event. He began to read the Bible, pray and became active in church.

As the final court date approached June 25, 1997, we found ourselves in a turmoil of emotions, not knowing exactly what to expect. Trying to keep our faith in front of our fears, we put on our Sunday best and marched off to see the judge. Upon our arrival things did not go as planned. Our pastor from the church could not be present, our normal attorney was not present, and they had a change in the presiding judge. Little did we know that this would actually work in our favor. Pastor had given us a letter to present to the attorney, which he read. Scott had met all the demands and requirements of the court, and the records indicated that he had done an outstanding job. The court was petitioned to vacate adjudication of delinquency. However this was challenged and objected to by the states attorney. Our hearts pounded. Then there was a God moment. The judge looked at Scott and said, "The record shows this young man has done an outstanding job in turning his life around. He deserves another chance." The decision was final, the case was closed, and our son was free. It was a day to give thanks to God for turning our darkness to light, our sorrows to joy, our anxieties to peace.

Reflections

"How happy are the people who know the joyful shout! They walk in the light of your presence, ADONI" (Psalm 89:16, CJB)

Thank you, Father, for your grace and mercy, that leads us to repentance and your unfailing love, that accepts us as we are. Your joy that floods our lives with possibilities of a new life, as we let your spirit work in us.

~ Forty Four ~
WHEN GOD MEETS A BROKEN HEART

It was time to take my lunch break, but my coworker, who I usually had lunch with, was not available, so I took off on my own. I was looking forward to a quiet lunch and time to be alone with my thoughts. It had been nine months since my son was arrested and found guilty. Although God was ever faithful, ever loving and ever present, there was still a lot of struggling between faith and fear, trust and turmoil and courage and discouragement. I had many good days when God's strength infused my life, and days when my faith staggered, and this, was one of the later. I decided to go to McDonald's and ease my pain with a nice cheeseburger and fries. I was standing in line when a lady and gentleman approached, greeted me and got in line behind me. While I was waiting to give my order the gentleman came beside me and said, "I need to talk with you. God has sent me to share with you today." At first, I thought, *This is weird! What do they want from me? Are they going to rob me? Why would God send strangers to me with a message?* The host asked for my order, so I turned away and ordered my tea, cheeseburger and fries. I found a seat, and the couple joined me with their drinks. They introduced themselves as he lay his Bible on the table and began to share the message God had given him. I started eating my burger because I was not sure this man and woman had a message from God. I was more than a little skeptical; nothing like that had ever happened to me before, but it didn't take long for me to realize that God, my loving heavenly Father knew I needed something special that day. He began to share God's love, God's Word and encouragement that touched my heart in a very special way.

This man reminded me not to be troubled, because God wanted to bring healing to my hurting broken heart. He reminded me that God is The Great "I AM." He was with me and would never leave me no matter how dark the situation. He told me that God had seen the enemy's attempts to take my son's life, but His power had preserved and brought deliverance to him. He said God calls you faithful, patient and strong, with His strength. I thought, *How could God call me these things, when I am vacillating emotionally and spiritually.* He also told me that my son would be released from jail to the work center, even though his name was pretty far down on the list. He said God is going to bring his name up on the list, and I would hear something within the next week and it happened as he said. He told me that God had heard my prayers and seen my labor. There were a lot of other words of encouragement that were shared with me, but I could feel the power of God, His strength and His love saturating my mind, emotions and my body. I knew God had sent them that day, to bring healing to this mother's broken heart, to draw me back to His Word and His power to accomplish, what seemed impossible, in the natural.

He encouraged me to go back to the dream that God had placed in my heart and that I had written on paper. We are told in Habakkuk 2:2–3 (MSG), "Write this.

Write what you see. Write it out in big block letters so that it can be read on the run. The vision-message is a witness pointing to what's coming. It aches for the coming-it can hardly wait! And it doesn't lie. If it seems slow in coming, wait. It's on its way. It will come right on time." God placed a dream, vision and call in my heart many years ago, and it was not only written on my heart but on paper. God was telling me through this man that I needed to go back and read it, pray over it and step out in faith to see it accomplished. This man went on to say that all the things from the past ten to twelve years would be worked together for our good and build in us a great faith that would be needed to carry out the dream that God had called us to do.

I left McDonald's that day after a very long lunch, restored in my spirit, renewed in my mind and rejuvenated in my emotions. God had not forgotten me and sent a stranger to remind me. I felt humbled by this divine appointment and so blessed by the lengths God went to touch my broken heart and crushed spirit. God knows us better than we know ourselves. He knows when you are at your lowest moment and just how to speak to us and who to direct into our path and share a word and change our lives.

Isaiah 61:1 says He came to bind up and heal the broken-hearted I like the picture these words draw in my mind. I see God gently reaching into the brokenness; pulling together the corners of painful emotions, tormenting thoughts, the debris from destructive decision and the shattered pieces of our lives. He holds them tightly together, and with the touch of His love, His presence and His power He brings healing, peace and restoration. Although this is a process and takes a little time, there will come a day when you can look back and reflect on how God walked with you through this "valley of the shadow of death" and brought you back to His green pastures and still waters, where you can find rest, peace and joy. Trust Him, rely on Him and walk with Him.

My son was released to the work center just as the gentleman said, and I even remember my son saying he was not sure how it happened, so quickly. But I knew that God was working behind the scenes to make it happen He still felt like he had his life under control. But I continued to pray the prayer God have given me back in March of 1995, believing that God was still working to bring him into the Kingdom of God. I will wrap up in the joy and delight of what God has accomplished in his life.

Reflections

"Now let your unfailing love comfort me, just as you promised me, your servant. Surround me with your tender mercies so I may live, for your instructions are my delight" (Psalm 119:77, NLT).

Thank you, Father, for sending someone to me when I was at my lowest. It was like you were right there speaking to my heart. Thank you that your love reaches into the depths of my despair; reminding me you will not leave me alone.

Through It All

~ Section Three ~

LIFE LESSONS

Through It All

LIFE LESSONS

During our life's journey we celebrated many successes, but we also faced challenges, tragedies and catastrophes. When life throws adversity our way, we often find ourselves stunned, overwhelmed and devastated. It would be helpful if we had strategies in place and ready to implement, at the onset. Otherwise, we find our lives stuck in the muck and mire of life's difficulties struggling to get back to a place of peace, joy and victory.

As I look back over our life's journey, I have especially noticed the threads of God's faithfulness, God's protection and God's provisions. During the good times and the bad, God has always been present; whispering "Peace" to our troubled minds, holding us tightly in His arms of love and depositing His strength into every area of our life.

God has used my life verse to sustain me in the toughest situations, and I have personalized like this, "I'll take your hand (Kathy) when you don't know the way, or can't see where you're going. I'll be your personal guide (Kathy), directing you through unknown county. I'll be right there to show you what roads to take, make sure you don't fall into a ditch. These things I'll be doing for you (Kathy) sticking with you, not leaving for a minute" (Isaiah 42:16, MSG). You can put your name in those parentheses.

During my life's journey I have learned a few key lessons or strategies that have helped me face adversities and come out victorious. I have learned that implementing these lessons is a process. Think about what it takes to become a skillful pianist. They have to learn the basics, study musical theory and practice, practice, practice and practice some more. Did you ever stop to think about what it takes to become a professional football player? You probably need to have some athletic ability, get involved in a good training program, develop and hone your skills and techniques, find a good agent and above all practice, practice, practice and practice some more. *It takes fortified focus, tenacious stability and dogged determination.* You will get it right sometimes and at other times you may give up or just fall flat on your face. *BUT the important thing is to never, never, never give up.*

Hebrews 12:1–2 (NIV), "Therefore, since we are surrounded by such a great cloud of witnesses, *let us throw off everything that hinders* and *the sin that so easily entangles.* And let us *run with perseverance* the race marked our for us, *fixing our eyes on Jesus,* the pioneer and perfecter of faith. For the *joy set before* him he endured the cross, scorning its shame, and sat down at the right hand of the throne of God."

~ One ~
THE POWER
OF GOD'S WORD

I think the first example of the power of God's Word can be seen is Genesis. The Bible begins with God speaking into the darkness, of what The Message calls the "soup of nothingness, bottomless emptiness, an inky blackness." God instructed light to appear and there was day and night. Next, His powerful Word created the sky to separate the waters above and below. Then God spoke and the water below was separated by land, which He called earth. But His work was not finished, and God spoke, and the land began to produce seed-bearing plants and trees of all kinds. God then called for lights to come out, the sun to rule the day and the moon and stars oversee the night. Next, God spoke, and the waters were filled with sea life and the birds filled the sky. God continued His powerful creation by speaking to the earth, and all kinds of animals small and large began to filled the earth. God created human beings, both male and female, and he blessed them and told them to: "Prosper! Reproduce! Fill the earth! Take charge!" God spoke creation into existence. What a display of the power of God's Word!

GOD'S WORD DIRECTS
In the introduction to this section I shared the personalized version of my life verse found in Isaiah

42:16 (MSG), ". . . I'll be a personal guide to them, directing them through the unknown country. I'll be right there to show them what road to take, make sure they don't fall into a ditch. These are the things I'll be doing for them, not leaving them for a moment." As a senior in high school preparing to graduate and embark on the calling God had placed on my life and anticipation of the upcoming marriage to my childhood sweetheart, I was filled with excitement and apprehension. I remember standing by the window of my office practice classroom (my lunch spot) staring at a mountain wondering what this life journey would be like for us. Thoughts of marriage and ministry were intruded by imaginings of where ministry might take us, what would our life look like, and whether we would be successful in this journey. Would ministry take us to Africa (I hoped not) or clear across the county? Suddenly my thoughts were drawn to a still small voice, which said Isaiah 42:16. This was my lunch time and I had my Bible, with me, so I sat at my desk and turned to this passage. As I read the verse my eyes focused on the words "… and I will not leave them for a moment." A sigh of relief filled my heart and mind as I realized that God would walk with us no matter where our life's journey took us. He would guide our steps and provide for all our needs.

God placed Paul in my life at a pivotal time and showed me He had a plan for my life and the move from Baltimore to McCoole was in His hands. When we were searching for the first church, God directed our steps and guided us to the place he had prepared for us, as with all the subsequent transitions in our ministry. The threads of God's faithfulness, protection and provision have been tightly woven in the fabric of our life's journey. God's Word has been and will always be a powerful force in my life.

GOD'S WORD STRENGTHENS

"I can do all things through Christ which strengtheneth me" (Philippians 4:13, KJV)

"I have strength for all things in Christ Who empowers me [I am ready for anything and equal to anything through Him Who infuses inner strength into me; I am self-sufficient in Christ's sufficiency]" (Philippians 4:13, AMPC).

I have found Philippians 4:13 to be another powerful force in my life. When I was younger I can remember every time my parents took me to the doctor, for headaches, stomach aches or just plain not feeling well, the doctor would say; "Oh, it is just her nerves" and give me penicillin or sulfur. I think back to those days, it was the cure for every kind of aliment. I had lots of friends in my first few years of school. I remember my Mom saying I never met a stranger because she would always finding me with new friends at church, on the playground or in school. But when we moved to McCoole I had my first experiences with feeling like I was out of place and feeling like everyone else was better than me. I seemed to find the resilience to push through those feelings most of the time, but throughout my life I have always tried to play it safe and stay within the walls of my comfort zone. But as life presented me with new experiences and or I decided it was time to step out of my comfort zone to approach something new, I would have to overcome fear and push into those new frontiers.

I remember one incident many years ago. We were pastoring in Pennsylvania, and as a result of my creativity I developed a heart puzzle out of poster board to share the various ministries of our Women's Missionary Council. I was asked to share that presentation at one of our sectional meetings. The presentation went so well that I was asked to present at our district's General Council. I was honored to be asked, but the night before I was frantic with fear and very nervous. Paul began to encourage me by reminding me that I could do all things through Christ who strengthens me. He asked me if I knew what I was talking about, and of course I answered yes. He told me I probably knew my subject better than those attending the meetings. He also said if nothing else, picture the audience in their underwear. I began to quote that verse over and over again. I reminded myself that His strength and anointing power was more than enough to help me make this presentation. What I failed to think about was the 800-plus attendees staring at me and the General Superintendent of our denomination seated behind me, as I rose to walk to the podium. As I placed the heart puzzle on the easel, took my place at the podium and took a deep breath; God's strength took over, and the presentation went well.

That was just the beginning of blasting through my comfort zone with God's strength. I learned to drive in my early thirties pushing aside fear with patience from my husband and the strength and power of Christ. At age fifty I decided to add a degree to my life and career experience. I enrolled at The University of Phoenix attending the Warrenville campus plus six months of online classes. I graduated with a double major in Management and Marketing with a 3.78 grade point average. I have always struggled with my weight over the years, and with the strength and power of Christ in me I set out and successfully lost fifty pounds. I have learned my help comes from the Lord, and I draw on His strength to face whatever comes my way, knowing that God will share the right Word for the right time to give me what I need to be successful and victories in life.

"In conclusion, be strong in the Lord [be empowered through your union with Him]; draw your strength from Him [that strength which His boundless might provides]" (Ephesians 6:10, AMPC).

GOD'S WORD SUSTAINS

I found in my own life that God's Word is my rock of refuge, my hiding place and my strong tower (taken from Psalm 71:3). When my thoughts were a tangled mess and my emotions a towering inferno and my spirit crushed, I would go to the Word of God and find peace, strength and direction. I am so thankful that when my son was incarcerated, we were surrounded by a wonderful church family. But this was still a very lonely journey for my husband and me. The devastation was painful, and the loss and grief were indescribable. There were times when I could hardly make it from one-second to the next in those first few days and weeks.

The "what if" questions bombarded my mind. "What if I had done this; things might have been different" or "If I had just prayed harder, this wouldn't have happened." We had served the Lord from childhood and spent so many years in ministry with six different congregations.

We felt we had not planted seed to reap this kind of harvest. "How could God allow this to happen to His servants?" When the self-talk was waging war with my beliefs? I would open the Word and just go to special passages and read notes I had written in times of victory. I remember taking the Word, one morning and asking God to guide me to verses that I needed to bring me to a place of peace in Him. I was led to read Proverbs 3:5-6, (KJV), "Trust in the Lord with all thine heart; and lean not unto thine own understanding. In all thy ways acknowledge him, and he shall direct they paths." I believe The Holy Spirit gave me my own paraphrase for this verse and it goes like this, Trust in The Lord with all your heart and don't lean on your own ability to reason, analyze and try to figure this out, but in all your ways acknowledge Him and He will direct your path. This verse became my source of strength and peace in the storm and is still prominent in my life today. In the most difficult times, in our lives we are to cast down imaginings and everything that sets itself up against the Word of God. We need to let go of the doubts, fears and the cares of this world and take God's Word just like Jesus said, "It is written." The Word of God is not an accumulation of words shot aimlessly into the air; NO. " . . . His powerful Word is sharp as a surgeon's scalpel, cutting through everything, whether doubt or defense, laying us open to listen and obey. Nothing and not one is impervious to God's Word . . ." (Hebrews 4:12-13, MSG)

God's Word Empowers

I need God's power to face difficulties in my life I need His strength to face loss and grief? I need His peace in the midst of the storms of life and the chaos of this world we live in today. When I need deliverance from bad habits, wrong thinking or sickness and disease; I need God's Word and God's Grace to come along side to empower me.

Proverbs 4:20–22 (AMPC) gives us the following instructions: "My son, attend to my words; consent and submit to my sayings. Let them not depart from your sight; keep them in the center of your heart. For they are life to those who find them, healing and health to all their flesh." I would like to suggest a few things I have practiced to apply this verse in my life.

1. Start your day in God's Word. Ask God to enlighten the eyes of your understanding and journal the key verses and thoughts that stand out to you.

2. Take time to meditate in God's Word; *ponder* how this Word applies to you, *imagine* what that truth would look like or feel like, and listen for God to share His thoughts with you.

3. Practice applying God's Word in your life. Part of the learning process is doing it. I often remind myself that the power of the Word is in the doing. I recently heard a pastor say, You don't "get it" until you "do it." This is a process, so be kind to yourself, as you grow in the Word and the Word grows in you.

4. Pray God's Word; this helps keep it in your eyes and in the center of your heart. I believe that as I give time to the Word, it grows in me and brings His life and health into every area of my life. I often take what the Word God has made real to me, personalize it, pray it and watch God continue to reveal truth to

me. A few years ago, I took Psalm 103:1–5; I broke it up into phrases, personalized it with my name and appropriate pronouns and prayed it each morning. As God would draw my attention to a word, I would look up the meaning and explore other verses using that word. The Word and the prayer have grown in my heart. This is like digging for treasure, and the rewards have been delightful.

Two

THE POWER OF GOD'S LOVE

Picture this story! You've just finished a busy morning of cleaning the house and keeping three kids occupied on a rainy morning; now you collapse in your favorite chair to spend a few quiet moments relaxing. You take a deep breath knowing the children are outside playing; you take another deep breath, and visions of gentle waves on a sandy beach emerge on the horizon of mind. Suddenly your peaceful moment is shattered by your three-year-old son bursting through the door shouting with excitement over his newfound treasure, held tightly in his hand. You bolt from your chair, and sprint toward your child, who is covered with mud from head to toe. He runs and leaps into your arms presenting you eyeball to eyeball with a muddy, ugly wiggling toad. Not what I would call an embraceable moment, unless you have a really good sense of humor.

Have you ever felt unworthy of being embraced in God's love? Check out this verse from God's Word. "So, what do you think? With God on our side like this, how can we lose? If God didn't hesitate to put everything on the line for us, embracing our condition and exposing himself to the worst by sending his own Son, is there anything else he wouldn't gladly and freely do for us?" (Romans 8:31, MSG)

My thoughts were captured by this phrase "embracing our condition." We are not perfect, and many times we find ourselves struggling with fear, doubt and sin in our lives. We should be running to God for his forgiveness, but some of us turn and run away from God. But I want you to know, that no matter how far you have run from him, if you will just start to turn toward him you will find yourself face to face with God, and he will embrace you in His Love.

When I look back over my life, I marvel at God's love displayed in my life. Sometimes that love shows up when I felt most unworthy of having Him pick me up and hold me, in His arms of love and friendship. At that moment, when I felt like I have failed miserably, He embraced me in His acceptance and let me know He cherished and loved me more than I could comprehend. When we had no money and nothing to eat but a can of Grandma Brown's beans and I didn't think He cared about my desperate need, He sent a man, to our kitchen door with $10 worth of dimes. In my whining, anger and fear, God's love came knocking at that door, not in frustration with my lack of faith, but with a reminder that He would always meet me need.

When I was in bondage to jealousy and felt like I was in a cage battling a lion, His love visited me in a prayer room; He embraced my awful condition and reached deep into my heart, taking those emotions and replacing them it with His peace. When my heart was broken in a million pieces, His love, arranged a divine appointment to bring encouragement. God came into my brokenness and pulled together the painful emotions and the tormenting thoughts and the broken heart; He healed and made me whole in my spirit, mind, will and emotions, bringing me back to a place of peace, rest, joy and victory. When I was facing intense pressures, that were consuming me and I felt like a ton of bricks had been dumped on my shoulders, God embraced me in His love and taught me how to lift my eyes from the chaos and fix them on Him. He became a shield around me, my glory and the One who lifts my head high (Psalm 3:3, NLT). He reminded me of His love, gave me His peace and let me know He was with me.

I like the beautiful image of The Lord, as my Shepherd, in the 23rd Psalm:

> *"The LORD is my shepherd; I have* all *that I need. He lets me* rest *in green meadows; he leads me beside peaceful streams. He renews my strength. He guides me along right paths, bringing honor to his name. Even when I walk through the darkest valley,* I will not be afraid, *for you are close beside me. Your rod and your staff* protect *and* comfort *me. You prepare a feast for me in the presence of my enemies. You honor me by anointing my head with oil.My* cup overflows with blessings. *Surely your goodness and unfailing love will pursue me all the days of my life, and* I will live *in the house of the LORD forever"* (Psalms 23:1–6, NLT).

Remember in the darkest night, the fiercest storm or the hottest desert:

1. God Loves you with an everlasting love.

2. Always run to God; He is waiting to embrace you in His love.

3. God has exactly what you need and is willing and ready to supply it.

4. God cares about the smallest need and the largest need; just trust in the Lord with all your heart.

5. When you struggle and fail, call out to God for He is ever present, ever faithful and ever ready to restore you in His love and empower you with His strength.

~ *Three* ~

THE POWER
OF YOUR CHOICES

How many times in life have you said, "I didn't have a choice?" I think we often feel that way, but we do have a choice. Choices can be as simple as what to wear, where to eat lunch, and which direction to take to your vacation destination. There are other choices like what career to pursue, who and when to get married and where you are going to live that take prayer, investigation and consideration. In Deuteronomy 30:11–19 (MSG) Moses had given the children of Israel a set of instruction for enjoying life and blessing or experiencing death and destruction. Verse 19 says, "I call Heaven and Earth to witness against you today: I place before you Life and Death, Blessing and Curse. Choose Life, so that you and your children will live . . ." Making the right choices determines a good outcome, while wrong choices can come with disastrous consequences.

In Genesis chapters two and three we see a perfect example of what happens when you make a wrong choice. God had instructed Adam that he was free to eat from any of the trees in the garden except for the tree in the middle of the garden called the tree of knowledge of good and evil. Then the serpent enters the picture and converses with Eve by asking a question. Did God really say, "You shall not eat of every tree of the garden"? (Genesis 3:1, NKJV) Eve responds, we can eat fruit from all the trees except for one in the middle of the garden and if we eat or even touch it we will die. I can hear the serpent reply, in a cocky crafty voice, "Oh! You won't die. Why, the moment you eat that fruit you will be like God; knowing both good and evil." Eve looked at the fruit and saw it "was good for food and pleasing to the eye and desirable for gaining wisdom" (Genesis 3:6, NIV). and she made a decision that has negatively impacted mankind ever since.

We can all recall times when we have made wrong choices, but I am so grateful that God's grace, patience and love sustain us as He works in our lives, ". . . both, to will and do of His good pleasure" (Philippians 2:13, KJV). I believe that even when we make wrong choices we may experience the consequences for those decisions, but God is still loving on us and getting us back on track.

A couple years ago I was facing some intense pressures that were consuming me. I was feeling like a ton of bricks had been dumped on my shoulders and I was struggling mentally and emotionally to breathe. My thoughts were bombarded with fear, anxiety and doubts. My body was ravaged with the effects of this pressure. I became angry, negative, exhausted and overwhelmed. Have you ever felt like that, when facing situations in your life? I realized, that indulging myself in this emotional rollercoaster, was getting me nowhere and I needed to make a different choice. We like to think we can handle life by ourselves. We have all heard a child say, "I can do it myself," and with our words or actions we try the same thing with God. But God's Word says, "In all thy ways acknowledge him, and he shall direct your paths. Be not wise in your own eyes . . ." (Proverbs 3:6-7a, KJV).

I began to pray and search God's Word for direction. I knew the enemy was strategizing my defeat as thoughts of devastation and disaster filled my mind. One morning during my devotions, as an act of centering my focus on the Lord, I was impressed to life my eyes from the chaos around me and look up to Him. I decided to try this refocusing action, and it made a dramatic difference in my life. When feeling overwhelmed by something, I would take a deep cleansing breathe and lift my face toward heaven, as if I was looking into the face of Jesus. I would smile and thank him for the strength, grace and victory He had already given me. I would then say, "I am so grateful that you have this," and I would let go of the feelings or emotions that were trying to destroy the peace of God in my life.

A few days later He shared the next phase. I was setting on the couch with my husband, watching TV. He put his arm around me, and I nestled my head on his shoulder and looked into his eyes. Immediately a thought raced across my mind and a lightbulb went off in my head; I don't have to look up, as if Jesus were in heaven. He is right here with me and in me. Wow, what a revelation! I knew it with my head, but now it took deeper root in my heart. I came upon a verse that took the revelation one step further. "But you, Lord, are a shield around me my glory, the One who lifts my head high . . ." (Psalm 3:3, 5–6, 8, NIV). Now after reading this scripture, as I focused on His face I can see Him putting His hand under my chin and gently lifting my face until our eyes meet. I imagine His eyes looking at me filled with love, joy and compassion. I can hear Him reminding me, I love you, I gave you my peace and those precious words; I am with you always. Someday we will see Jesus face to face, but until then we are to center our focus as Hebrews 12:2-3 (NIV) instructs us, "Fixing your eyes on Jesus, the author and finisher of our faith . . . so that you will not grow weary and lose heart." The next time your feel overwhelmed by a situation you are facing, fix your eyes on Jesus. Let His love, peace and presence draw your focus to His grace, His power and His love. The things you are facing today will be swallowed up or absorbed by the gaze of His love, the power of His grace and the strengthening of His peace. Choose life and live in the abundance of God's blessings each day.

Remember—Your choice matters—Choose Life

1. Acknowledge (to know thoroughly, to recognize a thing to be what it really is, to take knowledge of) God in your life and in making your decisions.

   Ask God to guide your thoughts, to align with His thoughts, His Word. Choose your thoughts wisely because Proverbs 16:3 (AMPC) tells us, "Roll your works upon the Lord [commit and trust them wholly to Him; He will cause your thoughts to become agreeable to His will, and] so shall your plans be established and succeed."

2. Use God's Word as your compass when making a decision.

3. Choose your words wisely, because they are a powerful force for good/evil or life/death—James 3:3–5 (MSG), ". . . A word out of your mouth may seem of no account, but it can accomplish nearly anything—or destroy it! It only takes a spark

160

remember, to set off a forest fire. A careless or wrongly placed word out of your mouth can do that. By our speech we can ruin the world, turn harmony to chaos, throw mud on a reputation, send the whole world up in smoke and go up in smoke with it, smoke right from the pit of hell."

(Definition for the word acknowledge: comes from Vine's Expository Dictionary of Old and New Testament Words.)

Four

LIFE IS A JOURNEY

It is important that we remember that our lives are made up of a lot of growth and changes, learning and practicing and failures and successes. Just like a builder lays one row of bricks on top of the other, to build a building; you and I are building our lives one process, once change and one growth phase at a time. I have watched my eleven grandchildren from birth to toddlers, from toddlers to childhood, from childhood to adolescence, from adolescence to teenagers and teenagers to young adults and have enjoyed watching them grow and change. Life is a journey, and the people we meet, decisions we make, tragedies we go through and the successes we experience are all a part of making that journey.

In the busy world we live in I am not sure we take time to stop and realize the process of our life's journey, where we are, where we came from and where we are going. It might be because I am an older adult, but I find myself looking back quite often. Sometimes it seems like yesterday when my fourth birthday party was canceled because I had the measles, or the enjoyment of riding my bike, or playing Chinese checkers with my great-grandmother. I remember those school days and wondering if I would graduate, so I could get on with life. When my children were babies I wondered when I would be finished with diapers and then suddenly, or so it seemed, they were turning thirteen. I sometimes look back at the difficulties, challenges and failures I have faced in my life and wonder what I could have done differently and how could I have gotten to a place of victory sooner. But I also look back and see how the Word has grown, how faith has developed, and the abundant blessings God has poured into my life over the years.

Colton Dixon has come out with a new song and I encourage you to listen to it on YouTube. The title is "Through All of It." The chorus goes like this, "I have won and I have lost. I got it right sometimes, but sometimes I did not. Life's been a journey, I've seen joy. I've seen regret. Oh, and You have been my God through all of it."

I would like to share a few thoughts about this journey called life.

1. Don't get stuck in the muck (wet dirt, mud, solid animal waste) and mire (wet spongy earth) of life's disappointments, tragedies and challenges. I remember watching Tarzan when I was a child and he was always getting stuck in quicksand, until Jane swung from the vine of a nearby tree to rescue him from sudden death. God has given us the lifeline of His Word and His mighty power. Isaiah 41:10 (AMPC), "Fear not [there is nothing to fear], for I am with you; do not look around you in terror and be dismayed, for I am your God. I will strengthen and harden you to difficulties, yes, I will help you; yes, I will hold you up and retain you with My [victorious] right hand of rightness and justice."

2. Learn to *"Let go" and "Let God* have the cares of life. Luke 10:38–42 shares a story of Mary and Martha. Jesus came to town, and Martha invited them to come to her house. Mary sat down with Jesus and hung on every word He spoke, but Martha was busy in the kitchen preparing a meal. When Mary didn't join her, Martha interrupted Jesus asking him why he didn't care that she was alone in the kitchen and asking Him to tell Mary to come and help. Jesus responded by telling her Mary had chosen the best option and that she shouldn't get so worked up. When I look at Martha, I see she was anxious and worried by the cares and pressures of preparing the meal while Mary had let that kitchen work go so she could be listen to Jesus' words and learn more about how to conduct her life. We need to let go or cast the cares and pressures of life on Jesus and let God care about all those details. We need to focus or fix our eyes on Jesus because he is the author and finisher of our faith. He is our victory, He is our strength, He is our shield, He is our peace.

3. GPS—*God's Power System*—God's leadership in our journey—"And I will bring the blind by a way that they know not; I will lead them in paths that they have not known. I will make darkness into light before them and make uneven places into a plain. These things I have determined to do for them and I will not leave them forsaken" (Isaiah 42:16, AMPC). When I am reading the Bible I am always drawn to the "I will" statements, and this verse has four.

First, (I) God will bring or come with you: who—the blind, and where—a way they didn't know. Have you ever been at a place in your life when you didn't know which way to go? Have you ever watched someone who is blind try to find their way? God is saying I will get involved in your situation even when you can see which way to go, and He will bring you. He will guide you, He will show you and He will speak to you if need be to get you to your destination. We need to rest in knowing that we can trust Him.

Second, *I will lead: who—those who are blind, and where—on paths they don't know.* Now God is saying I will not only bring or come with you; I will actually guide you down the path to get you to where you are going. God will offer you His arm and verbally and physically guide you down the path toward you destination.

Third, *I God will make darkness into light and smooth our the uneven places.* God will smooth out the path and turn the darkness into light. Think of walking down a dark path and someone comes along side you with a flashlight and all the sudden you can see.

Fourth, *I God will not leave you forsaken.* What a promise from our Heavenly Father! God is traveling on this life's journey with us. He is teaching and instructing, guiding and directing and working in His, with us and through us for His plans and purposes.

Five

I Am with You Always

Life is a journey, not a series of events that are disconnected, meaningless or directionless. My life's journey has been about the people I've met, the decisions I've made, the tragedies I have gone through and the successes I have experienced. Each turn on my journey has brought new perspectives into my life, and each acquaintance or friend has planted seeds of change to help me grow in God's love, His grace and His life. Each decision, whether right or wrong, has taught me to *TRUST* in the Lord, *HOPE* in His promises and have *FAITH* that He has the power to complete His work in my life.

As I have shared the steps, the places and seasons of my journey I was constantly reminded that God's faithfulness, God's provision and God's protection was always there to encourage, empower and equip me for the journey. Psalms 37:23-24 (NLT) tell us, "The LORD directs the steps of the godly. Though they stumble, they will never fall, for the LORD holds them by the hand." That verse reminds me of parents walking through the woods with their child on a beautiful fall day. They were holding hands and talking about the colorful falling leaves, downed tree limbs, rough terrain and the various animals they encountered when suddenly the child tripped and almost fell into a small creek. Fortunately they were holding hands, and the child was safe from danger. There are many times in our lives when we find ourselves walking through a rough situation, and what peace we can experience as we walk hand in hand with our heavenly Father.

I have learned though life's difficult and horrific situations to lift my eyes up from the situation and focus my attention, on the Lord who created heaven and earth, who opened the Red Sea for the children of Israel, who brought down the walls of Jericho and who calmed the raging storm, for He is where my help comes from. He is there lifting us up with His strong right hand, hiding us in the shadow of His wing and strengthening us with the power of His might. *Keep your eyes on Jesus* and don't let the darkness of discouragement, the fog of fear or the dense shadows of doubt blind you from His promises.

Life is a process of learning, doing and growing. You are not who you were yesterday and not who you will be tomorrow. God's lovingkindness and mercy are tenderly working in us every day in every way to infuse us with His life, which I like to define as His *Love in its Fullest Expression* We are constantly deepening our knowledge of God's Word and His will for our lives. Be patient and kind with yourself, as you grow up in the Lord. Remember, You are embraced in God's grace, God's power and God's love.

Reflections

"May the God of your hope so fill you with all joy and peace in believing [through the experience of your faith] that by the power of the Holy Spirit you may abound and be overflowing (bubbling over) with hope" (Romans 15:13, AMPC).

Heavenly Father, I know you walk with me through the good and bad, through the joy and pain and through the defeat and victory I experience on my life's journey. In you I find my strength, my courage and my hope for each new day, each new path and each new season of my life. Father, I know you see around the bend, so I will trust you and hold tightly to your hand; knowing you will never leave me not even for a moment. And "Through It All" you are *all-sufficient.*

KATHERINE VINEY

Kathy Viney has been involved in ministry for most of her adult life as she and her devoted husband, Paul, spent 25 years pastoring churches in New York, Pennsylvania, Iowa and Illinois. As a co-laborer, she has poured into and developed numerous ministries, enhancing music departments and enriching the lives of women and children across the country.

Professionally, Kathy worked in health care and the senior industry before deciding to return to school at the age of 50, earning a double major degree in management and marketing. This degree would lead her to a more than seven year directorship of a marketing and sales department before her final retirement in 2015.

Kathy's life journey is a testament to her own passion: "to instruct, inspire and encourage others to be the best they can be and never give up on their dreams." Her LifeHuddles Workshops and Seminars teach strategies for life as she boldly and humbly shares her own life's journey—from tragedy to triumph—from defeat to victory—from struggle to peace, presenting keys she has learned to "win at life," no matter what.

She and her childhood sweetheart of over 46 years have been blessed with three wonderful children and eleven precious grandchildren.

Life Huddles

LifeHuddles was born out of my own experience with challenges and tragedies. In the struggle to regain my equilibrium, I have discovered strategies that took me from tragedy to triumph, conflict to peace and defeat to success. When life throws adversity in our path we must know how to appropriate these strategies, to maintain our peace of mind and our wining edge.

I have found that God's Word is not only His manual for how I should live my life but His Word is the weapons we are to use in accessing and maintaining the Victory He won for us on the Cross. When Jesus was tempted in the wilderness, what did he say in responding to each temptation? "It is Written." (Matthew 4:1-11)

Lifehuddles
Educate ~ Equip ~ Empower
Building Strategies For Life
By Huddling Around God's Word

- To learn what is written and how to apply it in our lives

- To learn about His promises

- To learn how to be poised toward victory in our lives

- To learn how to use The Word, as our powerful weapon against the schemes and trick of the enemy

To discover strategies, develop games plans and deploy tactics successfully.

LifeHuddles Logo

LifeHuddles is learning how to huddle around God's Word and build strategies to win in Life. Huddles are used in sports, so the players can hear the strategy, for the next play. This photo shows some of my Grandchildren huddling around God's Word. It is priceless to see the next generation learning strategies, that will empower them, to lead a successful and victorious life.